THE U.S. NAVAL INSTITUTE ON

LEADERSHIP ETHICS

U.S. NAVAL INSTITUTE
W H E E L   B O O K S

In the U.S. Navy, "Wheel Books" were once found in the uniform pockets of every junior and many senior petty officers. Each small notebook was unique to the Sailor carrying it, but all had in common a collection of data and wisdom that the individual deemed useful in the effective execution of his or her duties. Often used as a substitute for experience among neophytes and as a portable library of reference information for more experienced personnel, those weathered pages contained everything from the time of the next tide, to leadership hints from a respected chief petty officer, to the color coding of the phone-and-distance line used in underway replenishments.

In that same tradition, U.S. Naval Institute Wheel Books provide supplemental information, pragmatic advice, and cogent analysis on topics important to all naval professionals. Drawn from the U.S. Naval Institute's vast archives, the series combines articles from the Institute's flagship publication *Proceedings*, as well as selections from the oral history collection and from Naval Institute Press books, to create unique guides on a wide array of fundamental professional subjects.

THE U.S. NAVAL INSTITUTE ON
LEADERSHIP ETHICS

EDITED BY TIMOTHY J. DEMY

NAVAL INSTITUTE PRESS
Annapolis, Maryland

Naval Institute Press
291 Wood Road
Annapolis, MD 21402

Library of Congress Cataloging-in-Publication Data is available.
ISBN: 978-1-68247-006-0 (paperback)
ISBN: 978-1-68247-021-3 (eBook)

♾ Print editions meet the requirements of ANSI/NISO z39.48–1992
(Permanence of Paper). Printed in the United States of America.

25 24 23 22 21 20 19 18 17   9 8 7 6 5 4 3 2 1
First printing

CONTENTS

EDITOR'S NOTE

Because this book is an anthology, containing documents from different time periods, the selections included here are subject to varying styles and conventions. Other variables are introduced by the evolving nature of the Naval Institute's publication practices. For those reasons, certain editorial decisions were required in order to avoid introducing confusion or inconsistencies and to expedite the process of assembling these sometimes disparate pieces.

Gender

Many of the included selections were written when the armed forces were primarily a male domain and so adhere to purely masculine references. I have chosen to leave the original language intact in these documents for the sake of authenticity and to avoid the complications that can arise when trying to make anachronistic adjustments. So readers are asked to "translate" (converting the ubiquitous "he" to "he or she" and "his" to "her or his" as required) and, while doing so, to celebrate the progress that we have made in these matters in more recent times.

Author "Biographies"

Another problem arises when considering biographical information of the various authors whose works make up this special collection. Some of the selections included in this anthology were originally accompanied by biographical information about their authors. Others were not. Those "biographies" that do exist vary a great deal in terms of length and depth, some amounting to a single sentence pertaining to the author's current duty station, others consisting of several paragraphs that cover the author's career. Because of these uneven variables, and because as a general rule we are more interested in what these authors have to say than who they are or were, I have chosen to even the playing field by foregoing accompanying "biographies."

Ranks

I have retained the ranks of the authors *at the time of their publication*. As noted above, some of the authors wrote early in their careers, and the sagacity of their earlier contributions says much about the individuals, about the significance of the Naval Institute's forum, and about the importance of writing to the naval services—something that is sometimes underappreciated.

Other Anomalies

Readers may detect some inconsistencies in editorial style, reflecting staff changes at the Naval Institute, evolving practices in publishing itself, and various other factors not always identifiable. Some of the selections will include citational support, others will not. Authors sometimes coined their own words and occasionally violated traditional style conventions. *Bottom line*: with the exception of the removal of some extraneous materials (such as section numbers from book excerpts) and the conversion to a consistent font and overall design, these articles and excerpts appear as they originally did when first published.

INTRODUCTION

Good leaders are ethical leaders. "I don't see what the big deal about ethics is," declared a senior officer to a colleague of the editor recently. That is both unfortunate and unprofessional. In part, the answer to the "big deal" is that naval leadership ethics is about the "special trust and confidence" entrusted to leaders in the profession of arms. Every member of the armed services has taken an oath and solemnly affirmed "to support and defend the Constitution of the United States against all enemies, foreign and domestic." It is an oath that is sworn individually. It is a personal oath and a professional oath, and part of the enormous trust given to military professionals by the people of our nation is a trust that leaders will be ethical leaders.

A 2014 document written by Vice Admiral Walter E. "Ted" Carter Jr., then rear admiral and president of the Naval War College, titled "Ethics in the U.S. Navy" succinctly presents the necessity of ethical leadership in the profession of arms:

> Our profession is unique. As a Service in our Nation's Department of Defense we are trusted to be experts in the profession of arms. We operate with lethal force and are expected to prevail under conditions of extreme adversity; in peacetime, through crisis and war. We build winning teams to deliver on this expectation and believe *warfighting first* accurately captures our priorities. The missions we are regularly

asked to perform, and must be ready to perform, together with the lives of those we are charged to lead, demand a trust in our leadership to employ every means available to make the right decisions. These means include a strong ethical foundation.[1]

The uniqueness of the profession of arms requires that its members proactively enhance themselves and the profession in which they serve. It does not require that every individual have the same background, opinions, experiences, or aspirations. Diversity precludes such narrowness. There will be different viewpoints and understandings of ethical issues and points of leadership. But no one argues that there should be no ethics or no leadership. No one dismisses the need for integrity. Just because a "right" answer is unclear, it does not follow that wrong answers are unclear. Leadership requires many attributes, among them, wisdom.

The articles presented in this collection are about ethics and naval leadership. However, readers will not fail to see in them a conviction by the authors that personal integrity is a foundation or core attribute of leadership and ethics in the naval profession. Integrity is a common theme throughout the articles. Interestingly, and encouragingly for the profession of arms, many of the articles were written by junior officers (JOs) when first penned.

Naval leadership ethics is about attitudes, actions, and activities. It spans the spectrum of military ethics and warfare but it always begins with the individual leader and his or her decisions and actions. The nineteenth-century Prussian general and strategist Carl von Clausewitz keenly observed: "Military activity is never directed against material force alone; it is always aimed simultaneously at the *moral* forces which give it life, and the two cannot be separated."[2] He then follows this immediately with: "But moral values can only be perceived by the inner eye, which differs in each person, and is often different in the same person at different times."[3] He is not arguing for situational ethics or ethical and moral relativism. Rather, he is reminding readers that moral values cannot be ignored in war and that the tragedies and traumas of war create some of the most difficult circumstances known in which one must make ethical decisions.

One page earlier in his classic text *On War*, he noted that "theory becomes infinitely more difficult as soon as it touches the realm of moral values."[4] It is precisely in such a realm, the realm of warfare, that naval leaders are called upon to serve and lead.

The American people expect that naval leaders with a strong ethical compass will navigate in the tempestuous waters of the present and the future and there is little reason to think that such will not be the case. The essays presented in this volume are given to readers, not as a challenge or an admonishment, but as pieces worthy of reflection, discussion, and debate. To the extent that they are used in this manner, readers will strengthen not only themselves, but also the profession in which they serve.

Notes

1. Walter E. Carter Jr., "Ethics in the Navy" (U.S. Naval War College, 2014), 3.
2. Carl von Clausewitz, *On War*, ed. and trans. by Michael Howard and Peter Paret (Princeton: Princeton University Press, 1976), 137 (Book 2, Chapter 2).
3. Ibid.
4. Ibid., 136.

1 "LEADERSHIP FORUM: INTEGRITY"

ADM Arleigh A. Burke, USN (Ret.)

When Admiral Arleigh Burke died in 1996 he requested that his tombstone bear the simple epitaph "Sailor." Throughout forty-two years of distinguished service Admiral Burke epitomized naval leadership ethics. In this essay, he contends that integrity must be at the core of professional ethics and presciently observes that a diverse and multicultural world and military produces a multiplicity of concepts of ideas and definitions regarding integrity. "Development of integrity depends primarily on the individual" and "individuals are responsible for their own integrity." Thus, there is a relationship between the personal ethics of a leader and the professional ethics of the leader, but it is one that must be determined by every person. The reading shows that there is strong continuity of thought and example in the Navy's history with respect to leadership and ethics. The two are inextricably linked and have long been part of military professionalism.

"LEADERSHIP FORUM: INTEGRITY"

By ADM Arleigh A. Burke, USN (Ret.), U.S. Naval Institute
Proceedings (October 1985): 116–19.

> *First you find yourself overlooking small infractions that you would have
> corrected on the spot in the past.*
>
> *Soon, you are a participant in these infractions. "After all," you say,
> "Everybody's doing it."*
>
> *All too soon you find yourself trapped: You no longer can stand on a
> favorite principle because you have strayed from it.*
>
> *Finding no way out, you begin to rationalize, and then you are hooked.*
>
> *The important fact is, the men who travel the path outlined above
> have misused the very basic quality and characteristic expected of a profes-
> sional military man, or any other professional man for that matter:*
>
> *They have compromised their integrity.*

This quotation, from a plaque hanging in the office of the Chief of Staff,
Marine Corps Development and Education Command, Quantico, Virginia, is
remarkable in its simplicity and truthfulness. My old college dictionary defines
integrity as 1: an unimpaired condition; soundness 2: adherence to a code of
moral, artistic, or other values 3: the quality or state of being complete or undi-
vided; completeness. As synonyms, it lists honesty and unity.

These are good definitions, but they are not very exact. They allow a great
deal of leeway because the descriptive words may mean different things to different societies, different cultures, and different people. What is integrity for
a Japanese may not be so for an Iranian. What is integrity for a cowboy may
not be considered integrity by a minister (the disposition of horse thieves, for
example). Integrity also varies widely among individuals in the same group.
Probably no two individuals have the same ideas about all aspects of integrity.
The point is, there exists no absolute definition of integrity.

Since no two people have the same values, how does a person acquire
integrity, a code of conduct, a set of standards by which they live? How does

a person develop a sense of obligation toward others, whether they make up a civic group, a military service, or a country? Most individuals' standards are learned when they are very young, from family, associates, and other contacts, from reading, and from watching television. It is well to remember, though, that families with high standards have had children who rejected the beliefs of their families and turned out to be first class scoundrels. The reverse is also true. People with integrity have come from families that have lacked it. Perhaps this does not happen often, but it does happen. The point is that it is impossible to guarantee that any one person will acquire integrity. Development of integrity depends primarily on the individual.

There will be wayward priests, crooked politicians, and wicked naval officers. In a highly moral organization, people who fall below the standard will eventually be recognized and removed from the organization. In an organization of lower standards, they may be punished but still tolerated. In an immoral organization, such as in a criminal family, they will be measured by their contribution to their organization.

Individuals are responsible for their own integrity. They will be influenced by many people and events, but in the end, their integrity quotient is of their own making. People are responsible for establishing their own standards, and their choices determine the kind of person they will be.

The integrity an individual should look after is his own—not his neighbor's, his subordinate's, his senior's, or his associate's—but his own. You can try to influence people to accept your views, but whether they do or not is up to them. A society or an individual may force rules on others, but no one can ensure that integrity will be inculcated. Only the individual concerned can accomplish that.

The integrity of a society or a group is approximately equal to the lowest common denominator of its people. When the standards are lowered for an individual, the standards of the group or society to which the individual belongs are lowered. Sometimes standards are raised in groups, but more frequently, there is a gradual disintegration of standards.

Since the integrity of individuals varies, an organization cannot maintain an absolutely uniform integrity; not even sequestered groups can accomplish this. A general level of integrity can be approximated, but individuals may deviate greatly from the norm, even in organizations that try to keep standards high.

In these days of high-speed teaching methods, young people receive guidance from their families and literally dozens of other groups. They even are given computerized, capsulized advice. Developing individuals observe the people who dole out the plentiful and diverse guidance, and the observations they make influence their acceptance of what is right or wrong, good or bad. The following example is frequently mentioned in regard to education: If merit and capability are not requirements for success in the teaching profession, then young people are likely to judge that merit and capability are not important. Likewise, if developing individuals observe that people with known moral defects, or people who are known to be crooked or liars, are accepted in society without penalty, they might well conclude that integrity is not worth their effort either.

Still, individuals determine what convictions they want to have and what they want to do about them. They continually adjust what they think is correct, what they want to learn, and how much effort they are willing to devote to each subject. Individuals determine whom to like and whom to avoid, whom to admire and whom to emulate, and make decisions about what is important and how to go about self-improvement. Individuals also determine what obligations they are willing to undertake at their own volition.

Since individuals create their own integrity, it follows that integrity is not fixed permanently. Integrity is a variable in one individual, among individuals of the same family and society, and among different societies and cultures. Integrity may be changed throughout life as individuals determine what actions they are willing to take to improve themselves and their integrity. Deciding how much integrity individuals want to develop is one of the most important decisions they make, whether they are conscious of the process or not. The basis of all education is learning to make judgments. This holds true for developing character as well as for becoming expert in any particular field. Individuals' judgments on material matters can be based on what other people have developed, and so can their judgments pertaining to integrity, but the final choices in both areas are made by the individual concerned.

Olympic athletes have devoted nearly all their efforts and time—often their whole lives—to becoming expert in their chosen field. If a person wants to become one of the best gymnasts in the world, that person ought to start training by the age of three—or maybe before. Since many people will find that their dreams exceed their natural capabilities, they will make the sound judgment not to continue to try to accomplish the impossible, but to restrict themselves to what they can do well. The lesson must be learned early in life that very few people can ever be number one. This insight is part of learning to make sound judgments.

Individuals who get away with schemes not to mow the lawn do not increase their sense of obligation very much. When individuals decide not to make the efforts necessary to learn arithmetic or calculus, it is not likely that they will be very good in any profession requiring a knowledge of math. The young person who fools around at the piano, not really trying to learn, is making the choice not to be a piano player. If people worked as hard at learning academics and professional knowledge as they do at performing in athletic contests, it is probable that the world would be a better place to live.

It must be understood that a judgment on anything is not irrevocable, although action taken as a result of a judgment, such as hanging the wrong man as a horse thief, frequently has irrevocable consequences. A person with low grades can see the light, for example, and decide to become more proficient in math. If desire is there, most things can be accomplished. It takes more effort, more time, more determination to correct an original wrong judgment—but it can be done. Grandma Moses became a great artist after she decided to try painting later in her life.

Of course, individuals can alter their integrity. Too frequently the alterations are on the side of lowered standards, as has been demonstrated in a number of professions and in government. The crux of this is that individuals make their own integrity by reason of their own decisions, choices, and judgments, and they change their integrity by the same means. At the same time, people should make judgments on other people's integrity gingerly. The many different concepts of integrity held by different individuals, groups, and cultures should be treated with all due respect.

Some of the most vicious wars in history have been fought in the name of religion by societies that had very strong—and very different—convictions concerning integrity. They disagreed on what was right, on their basic mode of implementing what was right, and on their bibles or the equivalents thereof, and thus, each side resolved to force its views on the other side. Both sides were absolutely certain they had the monopoly on integrity, and that the other side had no integrity at all.

The extended upheaval in Lebanon is primarily based on different views of religion: what is right, what is good, and what is the word of God. These differences have been exacerbated by greed, desire for power, and self-interest. The Middle East (like a number of American cities), is full of strong and conflicting views on integrity and full of people who do not seem to have much integrity. Some Mideast leaders appear to be scoundrels, liars, selfish in the extreme, and generally without socially redeeming features. It is likely that few people in this country agree with, or understand, their philosophy, and that fewer still would stand for any attempt to force that philosophy on them.

Keeping our own integrity up to par is problem enough. We are responsible for our own conduct; we are not responsible for another's integrity. If we have made the normal number of correct judgments during our lives, we have probably concluded that we should not try to interfere with the religion of others or to determine what is right or wrong for them. We should not interfere unless another group tries to force its views of integrity on us or our organization. Then we must resist or the other group's efforts will appreciably lower the standards of our organization. In relation to the naval profession, in particular, the following observations are applicable:

- Integrity and motivation are necessary in naval officers, but competence in the profession is also essential.
- Good intentions are most desirable, but nothing can be built or done by good intentions alone—except maybe paving the road to hell. Performance is required. Good intentions may help get performance, but the required end product is performance, not "I meant well."

- Integrity, or lack thereof, is not always discernible. Many people practice successfully to appear to have great integrity, or more than they do have. They can fool many some of the time. But always guard against making a final judgment on another's integrity based only on his own statements or on what appears to be.
- Be wary of self-proclaimed virtue. Do not rely on other people's evaluation of their personal integrity. Perhaps if they had integrity, they would not be their own press agents.
- The marketing of reputations for integrity is a good business. Many leaders have made good livings allowing their reputations to be used to represent organizations with no or poor reputations of their own.

Despite the cynical tone of these observations, most people and a large percentage of naval officers are people of integrity. They are honest; they are reliable; they are professional; and they do have good professional ethics. Have faith in your fellow officers, but be ready if one of them is less valiant, less competent, or less honest than you thought.

All of us can learn from the past. As wise as Moses was, he had difficulty hearing the disagreements of all the people who came before him. The people wanted Moses to settle matters between them and make known to them God's decisions and regulations. His father-in-law, Jethro, observing that Moses was having great difficulty handling the work suggested:

"Be thou for the people to Godward, that thou mayest bring the causes unto God. And thou shalt teach them ordinances and laws, and shalt show them the way wherein they must walk, and the work that they must do. Moreover thou shalt provide out of all the people able men, such as fear God, men of truth, hating covetousness; and place such over them to be rulers of thousands, and rulers of hundreds, rulers of fifties, and rulers of tens. And let them judge the people at all seasons; and it shall be, that every great matter they shall bring unto thee, but every small matter they shall judge; so shall it be easier for thyself, and they shall bear the burden with thee. If thou shalt do this thing, and God command thee so, then thou shalt be able to endure, and all this people shall also go to their place in peace." (Exodus 18:19–23)

The point is that when considering weighty matters, an individual can be helped greatly by turning to and relying on others for support, for no one individual has all of the knowledge necessary to be 100 percent correct all of the time.

One question to be considered is, "What should an officer do when he thinks that a senior is lying to the next senior officer in the chain of command?" Certainly a junior officer who believes a senior is making a mistake—any serious mistake, not just a mistake with regard to integrity—should inform that senior officer. For example, suppose that the officer of the deck (OOD) has the conn, and he orders "Come to 080." The junior officer of the deck believes that it is an incorrect order, and he tells the OOD right away. The OOD rechecks and either corrects the order or tells the junior officer that the order will not be changed and why. This sort of exchange is common in the Navy. Usually the senior will ask for the junior's opinion as a matter of training, if for no other reason. Seniors do not want to make mistakes, and they appreciate being informed of an error before any damage is done. Thus, it is a good habit to question suspected errors in normal operations. An officer, however, does not often deliberately lie to a senior.

This example illustrates how important it is for a naval officer to have experience in making judgments. There are, unfortunately, no general guidelines that can be laid down for the contingency of lying. The appropriate reaction to lying depends on circumstances, which are unpredictable. If a junior officer believes that a senior is lying, the junior officer must ask himself questions. Is the junior officer really sure the senior is lying, or is it possible that he is only guessing that the senior is lying? Is it possible that the issue involves a difference of opinion? Could it be a question of interpretation? Finally, does the matter have significance?

The junior must judge whether the lie will have an effect on the organization. If the junior concludes that the senior is lying on a significant matter, and that the senior's integrity is involved, then it is the duty of the officer to tell that senior that the matter will be reported to the next senior in the chain of command as well as the reasons why the junior believes the report is necessary. It is particularly important for an officer to confront a senior accused of dishonesty or another breach of integrity, and to advise that officer on the intended course of action, before he besmirches the reputation of that officer.

The decision to accuse is never to be taken lightly. An officer who accuses peers or associates of any kind of wrongdoing knows well, before he utters the first words of accusation, to expect judgments from shipmates and perhaps from larger groups on the appropriateness of the charges made. This is in accordance with the old adage: "Judge not, lest ye be judged."

Therefore, when the junior starts wrestling with his conscience to make the judgment on where his duty lies, he should resist impulsive actions and even consider searching out a second opinion. Friends in the unit will likely take the issue seriously, or at least the more conservative ones will. There may be one or two who have noted the alleged misconduct themselves. I suppose that this sort of a drum-head court martial without the presence of the accused would come to a general conclusion, one way or another. Still, the final decision is in the hands of the originator of the charge, and that individual must make the final judgment on what should be done, no matter how much advice was sought and received from others. The decision belongs to the officer and no one else.

Matters such as these are difficult for a junior officer, a chief of naval operations, or a president. At the Naval Academy, in the year just before they graduate, midshipmen are taught the relationship between duty and honor: "We serve the country first, our seniors second, and ourselves last." The future officers are counseled on honor versus loyalty in the naval service, and specific attention is given to the difference between a professional and a careerist. These definitions are given: "A military professional is someone who upholds the highest standards and serves the country with unquestioning loyalty; the professional is not motivated by personal gain. . . . A careerist is someone who serves the country in the best way fit to further his own career." It is noted in this lesson given to our future officers that the careerist is more likely to fall into the zero-mentality syndrome, to be someone who would choose to cover up those things that might draw discredit to his own unit. The professional takes on the issues directly and does not swerve to avoid criticism. These matters are never easy for the officer, but he must take on issues to fulfill the obligations he holds to country, service, unit, personnel therein, and self.

As a junior officer in a battleship, I was once involved in a delicate situation that I did not handle properly. I recount it here so that others may not need as much time to learn when the proper action should be taken in such a situation. On a Labor Day weekend I had duty as one of three officers of the deck. My relief did not return to the ship on Monday morning to relieve me, so I stood his watches on Monday without reporting anything amiss. When the derelict officer showed up on Tuesday, he told the senior watch officer that he had made arrangements with me to stand his watches before he left for the weekend. That was not true. He simply took the chance that some dope would fill in for him. I did not do anything about that misstatement, either. Within two years that officer was dropped from the rolls of the Navy for a similar offense. Had I reported him the first time, he might have been jolted out of his expectation that there would always be some volunteer who would step in to carry his part of the load.

There is also the question of what to do about a "whistle blower." The answer involves knowing whether the individual has made an honest effort to correct the wrong by using the chain of command channels that are available. A clever whistle blower can parlay an error into something that produces publicity and promotion that is not deserved. Recognizing the media's hunger for material to present to the public should cause any person to ask, before he blows the whistle, whether all possible steps have been taken to correct the situation. The naval service is an organization made up of people, and people are subject to making mistakes, but it is important for the public to know that efforts are being made to find mistakes and to correct them. It is wise to wait before making a judgment until you know why the usual steps were not taken or why those steps were not successful. It is also wise to listen and not make a premature judgment. Every organization needs good internal checking, internal policing, and internal corrective apparatus, just as every organization needs an external inspector, an external check, and means for external correction.

It is suggested that codes of honor and integrity must not be so rigid that they are beyond the capability of human beings to follow. I believe it should be the personal responsibility of individuals to decide whether to report lying, cheating, and stealing, and that they should do so only after completely scrutinizing their own conscience regarding integrity. When a person steals a pencil, perhaps absent-mindedly picking it up from someone's desk, the observer should have the discretion to judge whether the theft should be reported. A person can dream up many examples and possibilities, most of them minor, when there is no doubt that a theft, a lie, or a cheating incident has occurred. But the incident may have been so inconsequential that an individual of good conscience could interpret it as not significant enough to be reportable.

In summary, we must instill in individuals a sense of personal honor, an obligation to their organization and other groups, a desire to keep their own standards high and to keep the standards of their organization high. This sense of honor gives real meaning to the feeling engendered from belonging to a "Band of Brothers," and to other nostalgic emotions that are essential to a taut, high-standards organization. However, an honorable person should have the option of determining whether to believe that others are honorable and of taking appropriate action in each case. The appropriate action is not usually reporting the offender to the senior, but confronting the suspected culprit with the charge first. What should be done must be individually decided at every step. A fixed rule that insists that a person never squeal on a classmate, a shipmate, or a buddy is just as wrong as a rule that says that everything that could be construed as lying, stealing, or cheating should be reported to a senior.

Likewise, it is also important to comment on the issue of "pleasing the boss." "Greasers"—those who play up to their bosses strictly for personal gain—do not last very long in the service because their method of operating is discovered and disliked, and they are discharged. But also keep in mind that bosses are pleased to have confidence in the competence of their subordinates, and that there are few subordinates in any profession who do not want to please their bosses. Bosses have been put in positions of responsibility and authority because their bosses think the individuals know what they are doing and what their subordinates, in turn, should do. What pleases the boss is usually getting done what should be done. It is proper that all officers of the naval service should want a reputation for contributing to the improvement of their service. There is nothing wrong with that. Every unit's effectiveness is determined by the way the bosses, and everyone else in the unit, do their respective jobs. The reputations of the naval service, the unit, and the individuals in the unit depend on overall unit effectiveness.

Since the boss usually desires a reputation for being a capable officer, including being a capable leader, it is laudable in a subordinate to want to please the boss. There is certainly nothing wrong in pursuing that trait, unless pleasing the boss results in turning in a poor performance. It is usually not too difficult for the boss to recognize insincere support. Greasing seldom works in a classroom, and it succeeds almost as often in the fleet.

Each of us must make our own decisions about the meaning of integrity. I suggest that officers who want to be ready for the difficult decisions of life study the great military leaders of the world, their similarities and differences. Frankly, there is no shortcut to wisdom. Rules to cover all situations do not exist. Each of us must find our own ways. Our ability to make the best decisions at the time will certainly be influenced by our knowledge of the past, our consultation with others, and our ability to "see" the future. At the moment of decision, we will have to use our best judgment on what we suppose to be right and what we in turn will do about it. Good luck!

2 "THE MORAL COMPONENT OF LEADERSHIP"

ADM Jonathan Greenert, USN

Shortly before leaving command of the Navy, Admiral Jonathan Greenert, the thirtieth Chief of Naval Operations, published the essay below encouraging readers to remember that "challenges and assigned missions are transitory, but our principles and core values are not." Using the moral compass with which each individual enters service, and calibrates in accordance with service standards and the expectations of the nation, allows leaders at every level to avoid the rocks and shoals of unacceptable behavior and broken trust. Admiral Greenert notes that "ironically, pressure to succeed can create the toughest ethical dilemmas" and warns of cutting corners to achieve readiness, mission accomplishment, or success. In so doing, he reinforces the reality that naval leadership ethics begins with individual integrity. There are no shortcuts to developing leaders with character.

"THE MORAL COMPONENT OF LEADERSHIP"

By ADM Jonathan Greenert, USN, U.S. Naval Institute *Proceedings* (September 2015): 16–20.

To strengthen the Navy's ethical foundation and contribute to mission success, Sailors must reflect on their principles.

We live in violent, uncertain, and complex times. The future is unpredictable. The only certainty is change, and its pace is relentless. While we face these conditions both locally and globally, we cannot let ourselves become overwhelmed by the environment around us. Every Sailor is expected to lead in challenging circumstances and we must do so with a certitude rooted in our core values. Our principles are the lens through which we lead and make decisions. They allow us to be consistent when we deal with any crisis. Challenges and assigned missions are transitory, but our principles and core values are not. The thoughts outlined here are designed to help refresh our moral component of leadership—something worthy of review, thought, and commitment. The intended output is a renewed focus on ethical decision-making and behavior, so that each of us can become the Sailors and naval leaders that our people aspire to emulate.

Expectations: What Our People Deserve

A higher standard of behavior is a hallmark of naval service, and each Sailor is responsible and accountable to meet it. In its most basic form, the standard can be described as ethical conduct in an environment of dignity and respect. That is a fundamental expectation of all Sailors by all Sailors. It is also what American citizens expect of their armed forces.

The Navy is a melting pot of talent. We are stronger for our diversity and the different perspectives and experiences it brings, but we do not all necessarily share the same cardinal headings on our moral compass when we join the military. A calibration and alignment are sometimes required. It is important, therefore, that each unit and each service member take responsibility for creating an environment that allows strong moral roots to grow and be sustained.

Integrity, the quality of being honest and having strong moral principles founded on honor, is the cornerstone of an environment in which moral development can flourish. This essential element of leadership is vital not only to sustain a climate in which professional Sailors can thrive, but to ensure the Navy can successfully operate as a team—we must believe each other and be willing to believe in each other. Integrity starts and ends with each Sailor. It is uniquely yours and can never be taken away by others, but once lost or relinquished, it is extremely difficult to recover. Integrity gives rise to unconditional trust: trust in the service, trust in equipment, trust in shipmates, trust in the leader, trust in subordinates. Each service member must learn to trust, but must also earn trust. Without trust, we cannot delegate authority. Without delegating authority, we cannot effectively operate the Navy. The service is an interdependent organization, and everyone must be counted and depended on to do their job. The pilot must trust the maintainer and the "shooter," a ship's captain must trust the officer of the deck and the helmsman, the SEAL must trust his teammates. Mutual trust and respect within the unit strengthen morale and team effectiveness. The opposite is also true: The erosion of trust and respect in the unit weakens esprit de corps and undermines mission performance.

The chain of command is responsible for helping to ensure that standards are met by all. Commanding officers exercise leadership "to develop and strengthen the moral and spiritual well-being of personnel under his or her command."[1] Each CO is beholden to a "charge of command" that captures this obligation and calls on leaders to build trust through professional competence, judgment, good sense, and respect. Strengthening a unit's collective character is part of the unique authority and responsibility given to COs. Since "to whom much is given, much is expected," the Navy holds leaders at all levels accountable for moral infractions as well as their unit's overall mission performance. The Navy's culture of accountability is on public display each time we relieve a CO for cause. We quickly notify Congress in these rare cases, and we do so to demonstrate our commitment to the highest standards of public service.

Maintaining high standards is not just the CO's responsibility, however. Every leader within a unit is expected to exercise his or her responsibility with humility, show the way by personal example, and act as a role model for upstanding behavior and decency. Leaders are charged with fostering a climate where ethical behavior and moral courage are encouraged and rewarded. Sometimes this is simply a matter of ensuring that appropriate decisions are made on the countless number of items in our daily routine—small moments of truth where you do the right thing. Exercising moral courage may involve being the lone voice of caution or dissent when a misguided group or individual—even the commander, CO, or officer-in-charge—places an organization on a bad ethical path. Leadership should be judicious with the use of time, money, and resources entrusted to one's charge. Leaders define and set boundaries, purposely shaping their commands in a positive way, and staying vigilant for any slippage in the standards. Experience tells us that leaders "get what they inspect, not what they expect," and that people will respond when others believe in them, and when subordinates have something to believe in.

Establishing a Moral Compass

One's education, environment, faith, and experience shape individual value systems. Integrity and trust serve as the building blocks that help individuals build an even stronger ethical foundation once they enter the service. Trust in the institution, for example, allows them to more fully embrace the Navy's core values of honor, courage, and commitment. Articulating values is easier than living by them. The Navy's core values are there to help guide your actions, because ultimately one's actions alone define one's moral standing. It is not just about knowing the philosophy or understanding the watchwords; it is about saying and doing the proper thing. It is about accepting responsibility, rejecting passivity, and refusing to be inert in the face of a moral challenge. As Theodore Roosevelt said, "Knowing what is right doesn't mean much unless you do what is right." It takes character to act on one's conscience and step in when something does not seem right. This characteristic is more important for a leader than technical knowledge and practical proficiency.

Establishing a moral compass and using it to guide your choices involves understanding the difference between acceptable and unacceptable behavior.

It means listening to the small voice in your head, your intuition, that warns against words or actions that might be disrespectful, inappropriate, or wrong. It means focusing on our duty, and not looking to derive any personal benefit from our activities. It means giving credit where credit is due. It means building one another up, not tearing one another down. It means being a good team player and shouldering your allotted responsibilities. It means being truthful about what is going on, speaking up even when it may not be popular to do so. It means acknowledging when it may be beyond your capacity to accomplish a task and asking for help. It means looking out for one another at all times, on and off duty, and intervening when necessary to protect a shipmate who may be in trouble or headed in the wrong direction. It means being considerate, fair, humble, and open to serving others, even as you set high standards and pursue tough objectives. And it means becoming your best self, treating others as you yourself want to be treated.

Making Tough Choices

Making the right choice is not always easy. Any number of hazards can threaten to put us off course. Some individuals can fall victim to the Bathsheba Syndrome, an occasional byproduct of success where those heady with power can start to feel entitled to more opportunities or privileges, begin to believe the rules do not apply to them, and then think they are not accountable. Numerous studies and anecdotes have proven that even morally virtuous people can succumb to temptations when this misguided mindset begins to form. Another threat to good ethical decision-making is the inability to commit to the institution. That is, the unwillingness to operate by all the rules, regulations, codes, procedures, and guidelines of one's service, warfare community, unit, or position. Every Sailor is expected to be "all in" on those requirements, which exist for the common good.

Tough ethical choices can be even harder when individuals are afflicted with apathy, complacency, or close-mindedness, all of which can be contagious if not put in check. Another danger is misplaced loyalty, which occurs when a person feels a stronger allegiance to another individual or sub-group rather than to the Constitution and the unit (institution). Misplaced loyalty erodes good order and discipline because it trades institutional trust for protection of the undeserving. On matters of ethics, the interests of our nation and Navy must always come first. This simple principle is in our oath of office, which we reaffirm at every promotion or reenlistment.

Ironically, pressure to succeed can create the toughest ethical dilemmas. Individuals and units under stress to produce results may begin to cut corners, comply less strictly with procedures, inflate reports, assume undue safety risks, or treat people unfairly. Those who fall victim to these dilemmas try to rationalize that mission accomplishment trumps all else, but the reality is that the ends do not justify the means. Good leaders help prevent "gundecking" by ensuring that subordinates are qualified to do their jobs, have time to do their jobs, and do their jobs correctly. That approach makes our tasks more executable, but perhaps no less strenuous. As President Woodrow Wilson reminded graduating U.S. Naval Academy midshipmen in 1914, "Nothing is worthwhile that is not hard. You do not improve your muscle by doing the easy thing; you improve it by doing the hard thing, and you get your zest by doing a thing that is difficult, not a thing that is easy." Our toughest challenges can manifest in tests of either physical or moral courage.

Moral fortitude translates to good actions in peace-time. It also builds resilience that enables service members to cope in times of war and stress. The quiet strength that comes from understanding that your outfit is engaged in a higher cause, that you have a distinct purpose and direction, and that your shipmates are counting on you is what galvanizes warfighters to confront mortal danger. Those who are morally centered, take responsibility for their actions, and have a pragmatic understanding of their place in the enterprise—and are valued for such—are the ones who can do their best regardless of the circumstances they face. We are inspired by men and women who commit themselves fully when the chips are down, do their duty, and demonstrate courage and self-sacrifice when it matters most. Exemplary leaders such as Lieutenant Commander Ernest Evans at the Battle off Samar, Father Vincent Capodanno in the Que Son Valley, and Lieutenant Michael Murphy in the mountains of the Hindu Kush all made a difference because they were totally committed to their causes.

A Conducive Command Climate

To strengthen our moral foundation, each member of the U.S. Navy is expected to know and follow the rules and regulations of the service. Uniformed and civilian personnel are not on this journey alone. We keep ourselves ethically fit through contact with one another. Units that take time to discuss moral and ethical issues are generally more prepared to face the tough times. Dialogue leads to thought and reflection, which in turn allow individuals time to grasp and internalize lessons, so that when tested or under moral duress an instinctive sense of "the right thing to do" prevails. Individuals are more likely to make proper choices in the heat of the moment if a command has created this kind of atmosphere.

Units that encourage dignity and respect for one another perform the best. Leaders who set the right example, invest in their subordinates, offer them opportunities to succeed, and build both their technical and ethical skills are the ones who succeed in gaining and retaining loyalty. A characteristic of a healthy, ready organization is that it knows how to learn, balances risks and consequences, and is as tolerant of innocent mistakes as it is intolerant of character failings. Commands that build a strong moral foundation into their operation are the most resilient, ready to weather the toughest storms. They also tend to be the most bold, confident, and accountable.

Exercising the moral component of leadership is essential for today's leaders. Integrity and trust are vital to our institution and the missions we perform for the nation. Integrity and trust act as the aft and forestays of our core values of honor, courage, and commitment. Think about your own ethical compass— use it, calibrate it—so you stay on course. Our ethics underpin our character; our character defines us and provides the foundation of leadership.

As Vice Admiral James Stockdale reminded us, "Character is probably more important than knowledge. . . . The sine qua non of a leader has lain not in his chess-like grasp of issues and the options they portend, but in his having the character, the heart, to deal spontaneously, honorably, and candidly with people, perplexities, and principles."[2] Think about this as you confront the challenges of today and tomorrow. When we promote dignity and respect and do the right thing regardless of the personal consequences, we generate a positive, lasting effect on others and contribute to mission success. Strong moral leaders have always been and always will be an indispensable source of power that enables our Navy to serve its nation as a cohesive, proud, and effective fighting force.

Admiral Greenert is the 30th Chief of Naval Operations.

Notes

1. U.S. Navy Regulations, 1990, Chapter 8.
2. James Bond Stockdale, "Leadership in Times of Crisis," *To Promote Peace: U.S. Foreign Policy in the Mid-1980s*, Dennis L. Bark, ed. (Stanford, CA: Hoover Institute, 1984), 43.

3 "ETHICS FOR THOSE WHO GO DOWN TO THE SEA IN SHIPS"

Dr. Nancy Sherman

In this brief but poignant essay Dr. Nancy Sherman uses her experience of teaching a required ethics course at the U.S. Naval Academy as a starting point for reflection on the importance of ethics in leader development in the profession of arms. Platitudes and prejudices or biases are insufficient for developing ethical standards and commitments of military leaders. What is required is a hard look at the moral deliberation process, including the roles of reasons, emotions, and experience in the warrior's development.

"ETHICS FOR THOSE WHO GO DOWN TO THE SEA IN SHIPS"

By Dr. Nancy Sherman, U.S. Naval Institute *Proceedings* (April 1999): 87–88.

It's the Monday morning after Christmas break, the first day of lecture in NE 203, a required ethics course for youngsters (sophomores) at the U.S. Naval Academy. After the usual flurry of administrative questions, we get down to the real business of the day. My task is to introduce philosophical ethics not as some antiquarian relic, but as the stuff of each student's conscience regarding the vicissitudes of daily life—sorted out, examined, and clarified.

The job is to open the curtain on the moral psyche, and see just what principles and sentiments lie inside. Which are defensible, which are problematic, which need constraint and supplementing from others? We may end up labeling certain principles Kantian, others utilitarian; regardless, they are familiar positions each person holds. It will take a full semester for us to make our journey, but today we begin—and the way we begin will determine how the voyage proceeds.

We are off to a reasonable start. The readings include a parable from Plato known as "Gyges's ring," a ring that gives the wearer the power to become invisible, so that he can lie, cheat, and steal with impunity, for no one will be able to see him. But the wearer also can do good works anonymously, for those deeds, too, will go undetected.

Would you opt to possess such a ring? Do you consider morality primarily externally regulated—a matter of being subject to sanctions, both positive and negative? Or is morality inner motivated, indifferent to external systems of enforcement and regulation? If it is somewhere in the middle, where in the middle is it?

The question is not a trivial one for midshipmen living in a highly rule- and sanction-enforced system of morality. And it is not a trivial one for future officers, whose stripes and decorations are the external indicators of their character and professional competence. At some level, each midshipman understands that being a person of character is quite different from being someone who acts out of fear of being hammered for some dereliction. In the day-to-day life of Bancroft Hall, however, home to all Academy midshipmen outside of class, the signs of externally imposed morality and authority are pervasive, and more than one midshipman in my class confides to me that he thirsts for a ring that might at least allow some freedom from surveillance, some liberty to see how motivated he would be when assessment of risks and rewards was not a major factor.

I see the classroom as a place to voice just such a thought. My hope is that there will be a genuine exploration of why certain views and judgments are held and a questioning of views if they are held for reasons that one discovers one can no longer avow or endorse. The point is not to promote skepticism, but to sort out and deepen moral convictions—to come to know the reason why honesty is so important in a chain-of-command hierarchy, why loyalty may have limitations, why the Geneva Accords give prisoners of war special status.

But all this requires clearing away some rubble. Gyges's parable begins with a question: "Why be moral if it doesn't always pay in the common currency of happiness?" After class, a midshipman cautiously asks, "Isn't there a difference between the immoral act of cold-blooded murder, or rape that involves assault on a woman, and cheating, where it is property and not persons that are at stake?" Might we use Gyges's ring for cheating, he implies, but not for murdering? It is clear that the other officer instructors and I have our work cut out for us. Those who claim that ethics has no place in a college curriculum—that everything one needs to know about morality is learned in kindergarten—either are born saints or are naive concerning the twists and turns of moral development and the miraculous ways reflection affects action.

The first day is a time to air moral doubts. Gyges's parable asks why be moral if you can get by without it? In addition, there is the common skeptical stance that morality is just a matter of opinion, of preference, of taste. Moral debates often have the feel of that old Gershwin song whose lyrics reflect our differing backgrounds: "You say po-tay-to, I say po-tah-to. You say to-may-to, I say to-mah-to. . . . Let's call the whole thing off." The more vitriolic the moral debate, the more one might be tempted to say it is just a matter of gut feeling and taste.

But this is not where morality rests. If morality were just a matter of what an individual likes or dislikes, then the daily moral decisions officers make regarding the welfare of their troops would be little more than statements of preference, such as thinking that tea tastes better than coffee. Any attempt at justification really would be just a rationalization for holding onto a position at whim.

But few of us really believe this. And especially in the profession of arms, it is all the more imperative that moral commands be grounded in conviction, in understanding the principles underlying choices. May one lie if it will help many? If right action is grounded in good consequences, then we have a green light to lie. But if right action is grounded in not manipulating people, then the light turns red, even when the lie is benevolent. What if the person being lied to is evil, and is bent on the destruction of good people? Is lying to save innocents a special case? Does lying to the enemy fall in that category? Only a reasoned discussion will guide choice in these cases.

But talk of principles underlying moral judgment often obscures the crucial role played by emotions in the moral deliberation process. As the course progresses, we address this point. One common picture of emotions that emerges from the class is that emotions are the enemy of reason; they are the troublemakers, disrupters, upheavals, and passions that steer one from cool, calm judgment.

This is far from the total picture, of course, and an important thrust in the NE 203 classroom is to show that emotions can be salutary to moral judgment. They are part of our capacities for moral perception, antennae by which we pick up moral radar. By being emotionally sensitive, we notice who is hurt, whether a remark was more cutting than funny, that a loss affected another more than we might have thought. Emotional antennae pick up what is morally relevant for response in the very way that the emotion of fear can give the warning signals of danger. We read others but also ourselves through the tell-tale signs of emotions—being anxious alerts us to a concern we thought we were well over, being fearful warns us that there may be real threats ahead, giddy feelings may signal that we are on the verge of falling in love. Of course, emotions can get the data wrong. But that just means we need to calibrate our equipment better, not throw it out.

Often, we feel emotions we wish we didn't feel. To suffer post-traumatic stress syndrome is not to choose a mental condition that any rational person would want to endure. But part of what we know about emotional well-being is that it requires that we acknowledge emotions, not box them up and shove them under the carpet. However much compartmentalization may be a necessary part of the warrior mentality, finding a time and place to decompartmentalize, to acknowledge grief and mourning, to be honest about longings to be with one's family, to not merely suck up pain but to seek solace, is crucial to developing a whole and integrated psyche. Aristotle puts it well: Morality requires not merely making wise choices but having the right emotions. One must hit the mean with regard to both.

An ethics course, such as the one now being taught at the Naval Academy, reviews some of these issues. With Navy commanders and captains as section instructors, the ethics outreach is substantial. Perhaps the most exciting part of my job has been to teach with officers who have themselves been bitten by ethical inquiry, and can now look back on watershed decisions in their military lives in moral terms they earlier didn't quite know how to formulate. In some cases, the assessment has led them to question their judgment calls, in others, to realize they were justified though didn't then understand fully their reasons.

It is for reasons like these that the Secretary of the Navy has established a new Center for the Study of Professional and Military Ethics at the Naval Academy. One of its goals is outreach, to infuse ethics into the fleet and Marine Corps in the way that we have begun here.

Under the Center's first director, Dr. Al Pierce, case studies in military ethics have been commissioned, and plans for conferences and short courses in topics in military ethics are being discussed. I have taught seminars at several bases as well as with Naval Reserve Officers Training Courses on campuses around the country, and am continually impressed at how hungry officers and students are for substantive discussions on ethics.

The example of Marcus Aurelius, second-century Roman emperor, shines before us. He was a man of meditation as well as action, fighting the German campaigns on the Danube by day and writing a philosophical treatise on Stoic doctrine by night. Not a bad example.

Dr. Sherman, Professor of Philosophy at Georgetown University, holds the Visiting Distinguished Chair in Ethics at the U.S. Naval Academy.

4 "WHAT WOULD STEPHEN DECATUR DO?"

LCDR Thomas J. Cutler, USN (Ret.)

In this personal reminiscence of an event while serving as an enlisted sailor in Vietnam, the author provides a reminder and illustration of ethics, decision-making, and professionalism. Using Stephen Decatur, one of the Navy's heroes, as a touchstone, he reminds readers that there is a historical chain of leadership in the Navy and one to which every member can add a new link.

"WHAT WOULD STEPHEN DECATUR DO?"

By LCDR Thomas J. Cutler, U.S. Navy (Ret.),
U.S. Naval Institute *Proceedings* (November 2005): 2.

I was in Vietnam in the middle of the North Vietnamese Easter Offensive in the spring of 1972, and enemy regiments were all around us. Many of our artillery firebases were under siege and several had fallen to the waves of North Vietnamese soldiers sweeping across the region. One of those fire bases nearby was holding out, but the commander's assessment was that it was in serious danger of being overrun.

Among his many problems was the fact that his classified material might have to be destroyed in a big hurry. I had a sizable stash of an incendiary substance called thermite that came in large slabs and in the form of grenades—ideal for that commander's needs—and I was ordered to take it into that besieged firebase.

As it happened, I had some time to contemplate my situation, and it goes without saying that I was concerned. I vividly remember conjuring up what I could to offset my fear: the sense of duty that Navy training had instilled in me, peer expectations, fear of court-martial, the possibility of personal disgrace, etc. But one of the things I vividly remember thinking was: What would Stephen Decatur do? This may sound ridiculous, but I swear that one of the things that helped me get through that frightened anticipation was the knowledge that in the past, others had faced situations as bad, and many far worse, and they had found the courage to carry out their missions.

Lest you think this is about me trying to impress you with my combat experiences, I will tell you that this mission was cancelled. Other men had to deal with far greater tests than I had faced that night, because the firebase was overrun before we could get to it.

But the fear I felt was very real, and I sincerely believe that I was ready to carry out that mission for a variety of reasons, not the least of which was that Stephen Decatur was watching over my shoulder.

Many times in my career I had to face difficult circumstances where fear, or self-promotion, or greed, or fatigue, or some other negative force tried to take control of me, to override my doing what I knew was right, if not easy. And in those situations, while I relied on my naval training, my patriotism, and the values given to me by parents, teachers, mentors, and the like, I also relied upon my naval heritage to fight the temptation to take the easy path. Knowing what others before me had been able to do under arduous circumstances was a powerful motivator when facing difficult situations. I truly believe that a rich heritage can serve as an inspirational force when ordinary people are called upon to do extraordinary things.

One of the things that convinces me that I am right about this is that the Marines effectively use their heritage as a motivational leadership tool. Yet, even though we often acknowledge their success at this, we in the Navy don't do the same—at least not consistently and not nearly as effectively. We've all heard the stories of asking Sailors and Marines when their respective service birthdays are and finding that the Marines all know the answer, but Sailors often don't even understand the question.

When I bring this up in various forums, I often hear the refrain "But we're not Marines, and we have a different culture from them." While this may be true, it serves more as an excuse than a reason for our failure to take good advantage of a useful leadership tool. Our cultures may be different, but that does not mean we cannot change. It also does not mean that we cannot successfully borrow from the culture of our sister service. There is precedent!

Those guiding values of honor, courage, and commitment that we profess as our core values actually belonged to the Marines before we adopted them. We also modeled our "Battle Stations" event at boot camp after the "Crucible" at Parris Island. Have we somehow grown thicker necks because we now live by the same core values as the Marines? Were we wrong to adopt Battle Stations? Are we any less Sailors as a result?

The Navy's heritage is every bit as rich as that of the Marines. Yet we largely squander a valuable leadership tool by failing to embrace our enviable heritage as they do. We can do worse than borrowing from the finest Marine Corps in the world and arguably the most admired of all the U.S. armed services. Let us not allow cultural differences or service pride to get in the way. Let us learn from our sister service. Let us find ways for every Sailor to bond with the likes of Stephen Decatur.

Lieutenant Commander Cutler, senior acquisitions editor at the Naval Institute Press, enlisted in the Navy at 17 and was a gunner's mate second class prior to being commissioned in 1969. A Vietnam veteran, he wrote *Brown Water, Black Berets*, published by the Press.

5 "CARING"

LT Jason Brandt, USN

"Is there anything that you need me to do for you?" This question, asked daily by a division CPO to members of the division, taught a JO an important lesson about leadership—caring builds loyalty and trust. Leaders need followers, and individuals will follow and perform incredible tasks when they believe a leader and the command cares about them.

"CARING"

By LT Jason Brandt, USN, U.S. Naval Institute *Proceedings* (June 2000): 66–68.

Vincent Astor Memorial Leadership Essay Contest, Prize Winner
A chief's unusual question at morning quarters teaches a young lieutenant that caring for your people is the best way to ensure the success of the mission.

The crew of the USS *Crommelin* (FFG-37) and shipyard workers covered the ship like ants. It was late morning and in the midst of a hectic yard period I talked with my new chief in the passageway. I had been on board for over a year and had gone without a chief the past ten months. Chief told me that I had overworked myself, that the division had the day's work under control, and that I could go home and get some rest. It was the first time that anyone on board had demonstrated concern about my own personal welfare. This chief took care of everyone in the division, even the division officer. I was so shocked that someone was looking out for my well-being that tears almost came to my eyes. I began to understand what Damage Control Chief (DCC) James Armstrong was teaching me: caring for your people is the best way to ensure the success of the mission.

A year earlier, I had reported on board the day before the *Crommelin* retook the Operational Propulsion Plant Examination because of failing it four months prior. I relieved a burnt-out Damage Control Assistant (DCA) and took charge of an exhausted division. My chief lasted for two months before being transferred off for medical reasons. The ship sailed for a Western Pacific deployment and the damage control chief billet remained gapped for the next ten months. Despite assistance from the other chiefs in the department, I made many leadership mistakes.

For example, three of my sailors stayed up all night to replace a sewage valve at sea. I reported its completion to the chief engineer and asked what to do about their current workday. He told me that for them to work a full workday was not out of the ordinary. Anything less meant they were trying to skate out of work. They stayed on the watchbill and worked a full day.

Another time, the chief engineer, my leading petty officer, Hull Maintenance Technician First Class Batista, and I walked through a compartment that I owned. The chief engineer asked why a bilge pump was not working. Instead of taking full responsibility I stood by while petty officer Batista took the blame.

Throughout the six months at sea as a new officer with no chief, I fell, picked myself up, and continued forward. The fact that I completed the deployment as the ship's sea and anchor conning officer, a qualified surface warfare officer, and an engineering officer of the watch while still wearing ensign bars didn't seem to matter. My sailors were exhausted and I was burnt out.

The interdeployment training cycle began and I was taught by example to ensure success by throwing as many bodies as I could at a problem. The crew didn't stop working till near perfection was met or the day of the inspection arrived. This implied rule of working as long as it took to achieve zero defects seemed to apply to every member of the ship.

Chief Armstrong reported on board and I watched him earn the respect and loyalty of the sailors in the division. He put their welfare first on his list and had complete faith in them to accomplish the mission. The sailors knew he cared about them and would accomplish anything for him.

Chief Armstrong did not use the traditional end statement at divisional quarters each morning of, "Does anyone have anything for me? Anything I need to know?" Instead he asked, "Is there anything that you need me to do for you?" He asked this question every single day without fail. When a sailor had a problem, he took immediate and aggressive action to assist. I could not believe what an incredible impact a few words could make on a group of people.

The chief knew of every problem in his sailors' home lives. During a busy yard period an 18-year-old sailor reported on board. I did not make the time to find out all about him, but Chief Armstrong did. He found out that the sailor and his sister had been in foster homes their whole lives and that he literally was on his own. That sailor gave his full effort because he knew his chief would take care of him.

The night before the second day of a major inspection, HT1 Barela and DC2 Beam stayed up all night working on repairs. Chief Armstrong came in the next morning and listened to their report. Upon hearing that they had not slept, he immediately sent them home to rest. The rest of the division covered the remaining inspection tasks that day. The chief knew that we could pass the inspection with two fewer bodies. The short-term goal of perfection for the inspection at the cost of his sailors' health was not an option.

The greatest gift that Chief Armstrong gave to his sailors was his unquestioning faith that they could do the job. He attacked and eliminated any opposition to this belief. He believed in them more than they believed in themselves until they did believe in themselves. His faith was the catalyst that raised the morale and productivity of the entire division.

During the brief four months that Chief Armstrong was on board he successfully revitalized the entire division and me. In the end he was transferred to a forward-deployed ship in Japan and a new chief was sent to replace him.

The engineering department began preparing for its final major inspection, the Engineering Certification (ECERT). I was flighted up to main propulsion assistant (MPA) with collateral duties as engineering training officer, damage control training team leader, and engineering training team engineering officer of the watch. Here was my opportunity to put to use what I had learned from Chief Armstrong with the Main Propulsion Division. I would make amends for my earlier leadership failures.

"Is there anything that you need me to do for you? If you need, you can talk to me after quarters or talk to Chief." I said that at the first divisional quarters and every day after. The first day I saw many bewildered looks from my new gas turbine systems mechanics (GSMs) and electricians (GSEs). Later, I would get some comments like, "Yeah, I want a raise." I would joke back, "Talk to Chief. He handles all salary increases."

Several times I got the information that counted. GSMFN Parker had his seabag containing all his uniforms stolen out of a friend's car. All that he had left was the one uniform he was wearing. I had 20 tasks on my own to-do list. Solving GSMFN Parker's problem went to number one. It had to. Anywhere other than number one on my list would send a clear message that I really didn't care as much as I was saying. I tracked down the morale, welfare, and recreation officer and the disbursing officer to find out what could be done. I called Navy Relief, got him a grant for $120, and found the location of the used uniform store. I cleared his work schedule and that of another sailor with a car to drive him to get the money and the uniforms. Then I did the rest of my work. I didn't tell anyone else what I had done and didn't ask for a thank you. But I know that the whole division understood that I cared.

I typed up my own initial counseling form for the members of my new division. It was not a bunch of generic and impersonal questions like, "What are your goals, and what can you do for the division?" Those questions have merit, but when asked alone seem to mean, "What can you do for me?" Instead, I asked the names, ages, and occupations of every member of their immediate family. I asked what tools they needed me to get them, what watch station training they needed, what schools they needed me to send them to, how many pairs of coveralls they had and in what condition, how many work shoes and in what condition, and what did they need me to do for them? I had one negative comment that exemplified the leadership of my predecessor: "If you treat us like the last MPA you will go down like him." I sat down with each person for 30 minutes starting with the chief and working my way down the ranks. To take the first step and make things equal, I began by volunteering the same personal information about myself that I had requested from them.

I found out that most had one or two pairs of beat-up coveralls and half needed new shoes. Nobody had ever asked, including myself for my previous division. I realized the fact that I hadn't heard any major complaints before did not mean that things were perfect. It only meant that the sailors had grown accustomed to wearing old coveralls. For an engineer who spends most of his time in hot machinery spaces it is filthy and demeaning to give him only one or two pairs of ripped or old coveralls. I figured out the laundry schedule and concluded that in order to maintain adequate hygiene each sailor should have five pairs. I went to work battling with supply for the money to get them.

I asked about the status of electrical repairs and found that they were slow because all five of my GSEs shared one Phillips-head screwdriver. I went to work getting screwdrivers.

I asked GSM1 Wickersham why his mechanics didn't have the tools they needed and he responded that they had been lost or stolen. I had toolboxes and locks ordered so that each sailor could be held accountable for his own tools.

Self-respect for each individual sailor was critical to forming a team. When I learned of a petty officer with computer skills I had him support my overhaul of the department training program. Sitting at my desk in the central control station (CCS), I heard a sailor call him "the MPA's bitch." I did what

Chief Armstrong would have done. I immediately got up, ordered the offending sailor behind Number Four Switchboard and corrected the problem. "Every member of this division is important!" I said. "He is, you are, I am! And if someone was ruthlessly putting you down then I would come after them!" He was shocked at the anger and conviction in my voice and did his best to calm me down and assure me that he understood. I know everyone else in CCS heard me and I never had problems with sailors alienating one another out of spite.

The greatest gift I gave to a division of low morale was faith. I followed Chief Armstrong's example. I believed in them more than they believed in themselves until they did believe in themselves. The GSEs had been harassed and belittled for the engines' electrical problems since I had been on board. They had suffered from poor leadership and were a beat-down group. I didn't know for sure if they could fix a problem but I chose to believe in them publicly with complete confidence. "My GSEs are the best," I would state. "GSE1 Griffin and his crew can fix it!" What an impact faith can have on a group of people and on those around them. I said the words with sincerity and conviction and backed them up with my support. The words turned into belief in themselves and others' belief in them.

The ship passed the ECERT in one day and did not receive an evaluation of "Not Effective" in any single category. It was an overwhelming victory.

I received orders and found myself turning over to my relief the same week that my division underwent a weeklong internal inspection called Division in the Spotlight. I had served on the inspection team and had witnessed two main propulsion assistants get flame sprayed by two commanding officers for poor morale and division programs across the board. My division completed the inspection with the best zone inspection the commanding officer had done. It wasn't because I was the best main propulsion assistant. It was because I cared about my sailors more than anyone before.

I turned over the division to my relief and gave the sailors a final counseling form for myself. It stated that this form was a tool to help me become a better leader and that their honesty was appreciated. It asked two questions:

What did the MPA do well, and what could the MPA have done better? The responses I got back meant more to me than anything else I could have gotten from the ship. Each and every form read, "We knew you would take care of us."

Amazing what some coveralls, screwdrivers, and a lot of faith can do.

Lieutenant Brandt served as the Damage Control Assistant and the Main Propulsion Assistant on board the USS *Crommelin* (FFG-37). A member of the U.S. Naval Academy Class of 1995, he currently serves as the Military Advisor for Land Attack at the Space and Naval Warfare Systems Center San Diego.

6 "LESSONS FROM OUT OF THE BLUES"

LCDR Mark D. Provo, USN

Since its formation in 1946, the Navy's flight demonstration squadron the Blue Angels has flown for millions of spectators. In this essay a member of the team discusses five lessons learned regarding teamwork, honesty, and striving for excellence. His lessons are a succinct reminder for leaders that mission accomplishment begins with the individual military professional.

"LESSONS FROM OUT OF THE BLUES"

By LCDR Mark D. Provo, USN, U.S. Naval Institute *Proceedings* (December 1998): 48–50.

Flying as part of the Blue Angels flight demonstration squadron, a Navy pilot learns about teamwork, honesty, and striving for excellence.

From September 1994 to November 1996, I had the privilege of being part of the Blue Angels, the U.S. Navy's Flight Demonstration Squadron. An outstanding organization with a 52-year tradition, this team was formed after World War II, when Admiral Chester Nimitz realized that many Americans did not know that the Navy even had airplanes. Since then, the Blues have performed for more than 100 million spectators all over the world, traveling to 35 show sites per air show year. As goodwill ambassadors, naval recruiters, and dedicated officers, they show the American public and the world the pride and professionalism of the U.S. Navy.

I learned many important lessons from the Blue Angel experience—lessons that have to do with the way you think about life, the way you fly your aircraft, and the way you help make the Navy team the best it can be.

Lesson #1: Be Thankful

During debriefs, at the end of each pilot's description of how that hop went for him, he says, "Glad to be here." It doesn't matter whether he has flown a good demo or has made mistakes on several of the maneuvers—he still says, "Glad to be here." The reason for this team custom is because no matter how bad a show you flew, no matter who called you names in the crowd, it is a privilege to be on the Blue Angels team and represent the Navy. It reminded us that many naval aviators would love to have been sitting in our seats. When the day in, day out, grinding routine caused us to lose touch with why we were there, "Glad to be here" was a gentle reminder to every person on the team that we were very fortunate.

To be a commissioned officer in the Navy or Marine Corps is an honor and a privilege. I joined the Navy in 1984 and served as an enlisted man for almost three years. I always dreamed of becoming a naval officer, and I am thankful for the opportunity I have to serve with and lead men and women in whatever missions the Navy asks me to do. We must never forget that privilege. Our commissions come with a price—long hours, family separations, etc.—but there are many men and women who would jump at the chance to be in our shoes.

One of the most interesting aspects of my tour with the Blue Angels was meeting dignitaries, politicians, and successful professionals from all walks of life. These people had it all—power, money, success—yet almost every one of them said to me that if they could have done one thing, they would have liked to fly fighters and land on the decks of aircraft carriers. What a revelation. Naval aviation, indeed, naval service in any community, is an honorable and noble profession. Be thankful.

Lesson #2: Admit Mistakes

Another important lesson I learned has to do with ego. Most naval aviators are type-A, can-do personalities. Generally, this stands us in good stead, but such a go-go, achieve-achieve nature also has a weak spot. As a whole, we do not like to admit mistakes to one another. Too many times the immediate reaction to a critical comment from a senior pilot is defensive—every type of excuse you could imagine. Early in my first tour as an aviator I found myself and others falling into this trap.

When I arrived to the team in September 1994, however, I found a very different and refreshing philosophy at the debriefs. Despite their healthy egos, these men all came clean on every faux pas that occurred on their flights.

I first realized this after flying a backseat sortie with Lieutenant Commander Doug "Dino" Thompson, a senior leader and seasoned veteran who had stayed on the team a third season as slot pilot. As we lifted off for the loop on takeoff, I was in awe of his aviation skills. He was talking to me the whole time he was making radio calls and maneuvering the aircraft. Although he was very relaxed, in his voice I could hear the level of intensity that was needed to do this job. I was completely mesmerized.

The interesting thing is that Dino was the first man to admit mistakes. In one postflight debrief he noted that he had not armed his ejection seat before flying the demo. I was dumbfounded. Here was this guy flying in a single-seat aircraft who had admitted a huge mistake. He had made this mistake before only God himself, but he came clean nonetheless. It made a lasting impression on me.

This honesty was prevalent throughout the team. Learning from each other's mistakes made us better pilots. Coming clean every day helped us build a strong bond; we trusted each other with our lives. It improved our performance as a team. It also made us better people.

Lesson #3: Always Strive to Do Your Personal Best

There is a difference between accomplishment and competition. As a junior officer, I felt like I was in competition with my fellow J.O.'s. It was not bad; it was just that I constantly compared my performance with that of others. I also got caught up in the competition between squadrons. It was easy to talk poorly of our sister squadron because it made us feel better about ourselves. After joining the Blue Angels, I soon learned that my paradigm was all wrong.

When I arrived in Pensacola it was apparent that the focus was to make the team the best it could be. Each moment of the flight demonstration—from the march to the aircraft to the walk back, and of course the flying in between— was videotaped for review afterward. During the debrief we painstakingly went over every maneuver, trying to figure out how to make it the best that we could. The only way to accomplish this was for each of us to concentrate on our personal performance.

To compare yourself to others takes you down a deadend road. There always will be someone who performs some task better than you and someone who performs it worse. If you concentrate on your own personal performance, however, and measure it against your own baseline and standards, you can monitor and make improvements in yourself.

Lesson #4: Teamwork

The whole culture of the Blue Angels organization revolves around the concept of team. In fact, during the application process I learned that macho, self-centered, he-man types need not apply. There were, of course, plenty of healthy egos, but the goals of the team were so well ingrained that all decision making was done with the team in mind.

During squadron meetings, every officer had an equal vote. The rationale was that with 18 good minds collaborating, looking at a situation from slightly different angles, someone was bound to come up with the right answer. The Boss, just like any commanding officer, had a 51% vote and veto authority, but he rarely exercised it. Because any committee occasionally can get bogged down because of the sheer number of people involved, some decisions were made off line. But even those used the team theory as their framework.

Great leaders do not want personal loyalty as the number one priority. That takes away from the synergy of the group. Instead, they want loyalty to the goals of the team, whatever they may be, and loyalty to the team itself. This allows each individual to use his or her creative skills and feel a part of the group. Every decision we made was with the team in mind. It worked like magic.

Lesson #5: Teaching and Passing the Baton

As leaders, part of our responsibility is to teach our subordinates. Passing the baton to others who will follow you is another privilege that can and should be extremely rewarding. It certainly was for me while I was with the Blue Angels.

None of the new officers have any say in where they are going to fly the next show season. I was in a hotel in Ft. Worth when I received a phone call from Lieutenant Commander Dave Stewart, the lead solo and operations officer. "Utah," he said, "how would you like to be a solo pilot?" I thought it might be a trick question. "I'd love to," I replied.

"Utah, you are now Blue Angel 66. When the season ends you will be Blue Angel 6, the opposing solo." I was thrilled and scared at the same time. I wondered how I was ever going to do this.

We started flying following the Thanksgiving break. Lieutenant Commander Rick "Timber" Young was the lead solo, the operations officer, and my teacher. His goal was to make me the best opposing solo that I could be—and he was teaching a rock. I must have attempted 200 inverted roll-ins before I completed one where my wings were level on the horizon. This was just a basic maneuver. From there we went on to much more complex maneuvers that required hours and hours of practice to perform competently. Timber was with me every step of the way. He didn't yell or scream. He taught in a gentle manner that gave me the confidence to push myself and continually lower the limbo stick.

By the end of the 1995 season, it was time for Timber to hand the baton to me and let me have the privilege of teaching the new opposing solo, Lieutenant Ryan "Doc" Scholl. Passing the baton to Doc was a joy. He worked diligently, kept his mouth closed and ears open, and soaked up all that I was able to bring to the table. I learned many lessons from him as well. It was a partnership of peers.

Doc and I reached all of our goals except one. The tuckover roll was the most difficult for us to perform and we never flew the perfect one.

That would have been the end of my Blue Angels experience had not the new opposing solo injured himself and been unable to fly for the first few weeks of the 1997 season. I came back to the team as Number 6 for the first two air shows.

It was great to get the chance to see the student be the teacher. Doc taught me many new techniques that helped us have the tightest solo program that we were capable of doing. At the first air show of the season in El Centro, California, I could tell that the hop was going to be our best effort ever. When we sat down later to watch the video debrief, the elusive tuckover roll that had plagued us for so long was the last solo maneuver to be played. As we watched it the whole room smiled. It took us two plus years, but we had accomplished our elusive goal: the maneuver was perfect. I had passed the baton to Doc and he ended up passing it back to me. That day was the culmination of all of the lessons that I learned while being a member of the Navy Flight Demonstration Squadron.

I went back to the F/A-18 training squadron for a few months, carrier qualified, and now am working as the operations officer for the VFA-136 Knighthawks. On board the *John C. Stennis* (CVN-74), we have been flying missions in the Arabian Gulf in support of Operation Southern Watch over Iraq. Have I used my Blue Angel lessons in my new job? Absolutely. I am fortunate that the men in my squadron share the same ideals and goals. From our commanding officer on down, we are trying to be the best squadron that we can be.

Lieutenant Commander Provo flew with the Blue Angels from 1994 to 1997. He is operations officer for VFA-136 at NAS Oceana, Virginia.

7 "THERE IS NO GRAY AREA"

LT David S. Kemp, USN

This article was awarded Second Co-Honorable Mention in the Vincent Astor Memorial Leadership Contest in 1997, and the thoughts in it are as applicable today as they were twenty years ago. Arguing "there is no gray area between right and wrong," Lieutenant Kemp illustrates his thesis with a hypothetical story of a JO faced with competing responsibilities for time and attention. It is a well-known and oft-experienced dilemma. His warning to avoid the slippery slope toward erosion of one's personal integrity and professional ethics is the most important preventive maintenance a leader can perform.

"THERE IS NO GRAY AREA"

By LT David S. Kemp, USN, U.S. Naval Institute *Proceedings* (June 1997): 53–54.

> **Vincent Astor Memorial Leadership Essay Contest, Second Co-Honorable Mention**

What is the difference between a leader and a naval leader? At first glance, it seems only to be that a naval leader must wear a uniform. Further reflection, however, evokes other distinctions. The word "leader" brings to mind a person with good oratory skills who can motivate a group, such as the president of a major corporation. The words "naval leader," on the other hand, conjure up images of men renowned for their extraordinary exploits at sea. The phrase has a heroic sense to it, in which famous admirals such as Bull Halsey, Raymond Spruance, Arleigh Burke, and Chester Nimitz are recalled. These men of honor, bravery, and integrity were genuine heroes.

Recently, this image of naval leadership has been tarnished by negative incidents—scandals at the U.S. Naval Academy, charges of sexual harassment, fraternization, and removal of ship captains for creating negative command environments. Our first reaction is to feel that these things happen in all the services, as well as in the private sector, and that the Navy has been unfairly singled out in the press since Tailhook. This may be true, but as Lieutenant Commander Lori Melling Tanner writing in the January 1997 issue of *Proceedings* pointed out, our focus on simply the bad publicity is an ominous sign of where we might be headed as an organization.[1]

Rather than concentrating on the press coverage of these incidents, it would be more constructive to look at their cause—leadership problems. The Navy is experiencing an erosion of personal integrity among its officers, and it is having a direct effect on the comportment of its officers and men. It is widespread and contagious, and must be faced immediately.

A 1959 text entitled *Naval Leadership* defines leadership as "the art, science, or gift by which a person is enabled and privileged to direct the thoughts, plans, and actions of others in such a manner as to command their obedience, their confidence, their respect, and their loyal cooperation." It goes on to explain that a naval officer's basic philosophy of leadership "must be based on an impeccable foundation of high moral values and character integrity. . . . Personal integrity has always been demanded of U.S. officers, and in this age of rapid scientific and technological development, the leader must never forget that this is still the prime ingredient of the Naval Officer." Although the book was written almost 40 years ago, its insightful comments still are applicable today.[2]

Unfortunately, we have strayed from this noble concept of leadership. Today's junior officers are faced with a staggering responsibility when they report to the fleet. Although they have received leadership training during their entry pipeline, the real fleet is a shock. They immediately are confronted with a complex bureaucracy that they must master to survive; they must qualify, stand watch, manage complicated supply, maintenance, and personnel organizations, conquer collateral duties that often are more time-consuming than their primary jobs, and on top of all this, learn how to lead the men and women working for them. It is a daunting and often overwhelming task.

It is at this point in their careers that junior officers are tempted to start making decisions that can erode their personal integrity. At first, these compromises seem like small transgressions committed merely to survive. Consider, for example, the all-too-familiar situation of fictitious Surface Warfare Officer Jones:

It is Friday afternoon after a week of 12-hour days. Ensign Jones has just reported on board his new ship and is swamped. He is in a three section in-port duty rotation and during his duty day, stands port and starboard watches as the officer of the deck (in port) under instruction. There is a major inspection scheduled for next week and the ensign is trying valiantly to make all of the necessary preparations. With all of the activity, Ensign Jones has not completed a minor administrative detail—his weekly damage control (DC) planned maintenance system (PMS) spot check. His division's DC maintenance man has been waiting all day to perform this check. It is almost time to secure for the day, so the DC maintenance man knocks at his ensign's stateroom door. "Sir," he asks, "do you have time to get this battle lantern spot check out of the way?"

The ensign has totally forgotten about the spot check, [and had] intended to study for his officer of the deck (in port) qualification this afternoon, but is still getting ready for the inspection coming next week. He doesn't think he can possibly find the 30 minutes required to perform the spot check, but then he remembers having heard of other officers "talking through" a spot check—he has found the solution to his dilemma. He takes five minutes, glances at the PMS card, asks a few questions, never leaves his stateroom to look at a battle lantern, and signs the spot-check form. He rationalizes that he will do this just this one time, because the major inspection is such a high priority and he doesn't want to keep his maintenance man around any longer on a Friday afternoon.

This harried junior officer has just compromised his personal integrity by signing a spot-check form without verifying the maintenance. He does feel bad about it, and later discusses the spot check with a similarly overworked junior officer. They complain about the captain, the executive officer (who will "kill" them if they don't complete their spot checks by Friday afternoon), and the department head, and decide that the abbreviated spot check is not going to ruin Ensign Jones's divisional PMS system. They decide that what Ensign Jones did was in that gray area between right and wrong.

Wrong! This is how a naval officer's personal integrity lapses start. There is no gray area between right and wrong.

Our fictional Ensign Jones has just taken the first step on the slippery slope toward the erosion of his personal integrity. The next time he is in a similar situation, which in all likelihood will be soon, it will be even easier to make the same erroneous decision—the third time, easier still. Soon, he will progress to signing PMS boards without verifying them because he just can't find the time. Maybe he'll backdate a personal qualification standard sheet that he forgot to sign the week before. Each time he compromises his personal integrity in a small way, it becomes both easier to continue to commit small transgressions and more likely that he will commit a larger transgression later in his career, like signing a weapons inventory that he never performed or making a false report to the captain to avoid getting in trouble.

The results of these integrity lapses are detrimental not only to the readiness and safety of the command but also to the morale of the crew. In Ensign Jones's case, the young enlisted damage control maintenance man, who has spent hours preparing his spot check for his new ensign in an attempt to earn some recognition and praise, now feels misled and has lost respect for his division officer. He has performed a lot of work for a program that appears to be of little importance to Ensign Jones. The next time, the maintenance man will invest less time in ensuring that he has done quality work.

This disease of eroding personal integrity also is contagious. Other junior officers on board, who are similarly overworked, are going to notice that Ensign Jones always seems to be able to complete his work on time. They will discover his methods and be tempted to follow him into the mythical "gray area" between right and wrong, so as not to get too far behind this golden child. Of course, the example of Ensign Jones has been slightly stretched, but one can see that the erosion of personal integrity starts with small transgressions. The little things do count.

How do we combat this erosion of personal integrity? The solution is not as evident as the problem, but there are several actions that can be taken by the current generation of naval leaders to counter this epidemic.

First, we need to continue the leadership training that currently is provided in the various commissioning pipelines. The Navy's emphasis on the core values of honor, courage, and commitment is a step in the right direction. We also need to give our junior officers a stronger foundation in time-management skills. A junior officer who feels less pressured and less overwhelmed by his workload will feel more in control and will be less likely to compromise his personal integrity through shortcuts.

We need to set aside, especially in the surface warfare community, dedicated administrative time each week, during which paperwork can be accomplished without constant interruption. If inefficient or outdated administrative practices are still in use, the executive officer needs to encourage his people, not to ignore them, but either to try to change them or to request a waiver for the ship. This could be the perfect occasion to use the total quality leadership process, which, if managed correctly, will earn praises from the ship's chain of command. The fleets seem to be receptive to this type of administrative review, as shown by the initiative under way in the Pacific Fleet to redefine administrative requirements to allow frigate-size ships to expand from three or four section in-port duty to five or six.

The commanding officer, executive officer, and department heads need to insist on attention to detail. This is different from micromanagement. When the New York City Police Department, in the early 1990s, started paying more attention to minor crimes that used to be overlooked—such as littering, begging, and jumping the turnstile on the subway—they found that the rate of major crimes, such as theft, murder, and rape, dropped significantly. We will have similar results in the Navy. If we concentrate on demanding excellence and honesty in the little tasks, the rate of large personal integrity compromises will drop.

There needs to be more time spent together among the commanding officer, the executive officer, and the junior officers. Daily or weekly junior officer training sessions usually are scheduled during the Planning Board for Training, but it is easy for them to be brushed aside because of time constraints or higher priorities. This has to stop. This type of training and mentoring needs to be set as the priority for junior officers. The commanding officer must demonstrate that he is interested in the professional development of his junior officers. As then–Captain Kevin Green noted in his July 1996 *Proceedings* article, "Give Her All You Got," the crew will accept as important that which seems important to the captain.[3]

We also have experienced a real loss of wardroom etiquette, ceremony, and tradition in the U.S. Navy. This has become especially evident to me since I started my current tour as a Personnel Exchange Program officer stationed on board a French guided-missile destroyer, where wardroom customs and traditions still are rigorously enforced. This gives a young French officer a real sense both of belonging to a special organization and of the importance of honor and courtesy.

Traditions and ceremonies, according to *Naval Leadership*, "lend an air of dignity and respect" and "give to the officer corps its highest incentive to carry on." When you couple this with the manners, conduct, and pride that junior officers will acquire in a good wardroom setting (calls, dinings in/out), young ensigns will truly feel like officers and gentlemen and will conduct themselves as such.

Unfortunately, ironclad integrity and superior leadership are not as contagious as poor leadership or bad example. But if we adopt measures to guard against the erosion of integrity among our junior officers, we can attain the standards of excellence that always have been—and still are—expected of a naval officer. If the U.S. Navy concentrates on integrity in all facets of its mission and at all levels, including the little things, we will rise above our current predicament and once again be recognized as a breeding ground for the heroes of the United States.

Lieutenant Kemp is the Personnel Exchange Program Officer, Toulon, France, stationed on board the French guided-missile destroyer *Duquesne*, where he is serving as a division officer in the operations/combat systems department. He also has served as antisubmarine warfare officer, ordnance officer, and combat information center officer on board the USS *Reid* (FFG-30).

Notes

1. Lt. Cdr. Lori Melling Tanner, USN, "Do-As-I-Say Core Values?" U.S. Naval Institute *Proceedings* (January 1997): 68.
2. *Naval Leadership* (Annapolis, Md.: Naval Institute Press, 1959).
3. Capt. Kevin Green, USN, "Give Her All You Got," U.S. Naval Institute *Proceedings* (July 1996): 28–32.

8 "CAUSE FOR ALARM"

LT James Drennan, USN

When a commanding officer is detached for cause the action comes at the end of a period of turmoil for a command, a ship, or a crew. From a leadership and morale perspective, the damage is already done. The author encourages readers to distinguish *integrity* from *morality*, contending that "integrity provides the link between individual behavior and organizational principles." Just as a ship must maintain watertight integrity, so too must leaders at every level maintain personal integrity. Drennan encourages his peers (junior officers) to cultivate integrity throughout their careers and reminds readers that the American people do not have a lower standard or lesser expectations for JOs than for COs. Just as a breach of watertight integrity can sink a ship, a breach in personal integrity can sink a career.

"CAUSE FOR ALARM"

By LT James Drennan, USN, U.S. Naval Institute *Proceedings* (December 2012): 52–57.

The Navy's future leaders should go to General Quarters with so many commanding officers being in the headlines lately.

A young submariner once wrote, "It is integrity that bonds the crew of a submarine so tightly together that when faced with any circumstance, each individual can trust his shipmate to meet the needs of the moment." This anonymous sailor went on to make the comparison between integrity in professional conduct and the physical integrity of a ship.[1] It seems that officers in today's Navy need to extend this analogy to address integrity in personal conduct.

Now-retired Vice Admiral Thomas Kilcline brought the issue of personal integrity to the fore in 2010 through a concept called "The Whole Sailor."[2] Unfortunately, the rate of personal misconduct, specifically among commanding officers (COs), has only increased. In the Summer 2012 *Naval War College Review*, Navy Captain Mark Light sought to bring attention to integrity problems at the command level through an analysis of COs who were "detached for cause (DFC)" from 1999 to 2010. He pointed out that in 2010, 13 DFCs were due to personal misconduct, compared with a total of 29 in the preceding decade. Since that analysis concluded in 2010, 25 COs (not counting the most recent incident involving the command of the USS *Vandegrift* [FFG-48]) have been fired for integrity related incidents.[3] Whether or not these numbers represent a real deterioration of integrity among COs—or just heavier focus on personal conduct from senior leadership—a seemingly never-ending stream of embarrassing headlines ("Submarine commander sunk after allegedly faking death to end affair") and a desensitized tone from the public ("Navy Skippers: The Gift that Keeps on Giving") are unquestionably cause for alarm.[4]

To be fair, senior Navy leaders have not hesitated in taking immediate action. For one, the Navy has been forthright regarding the behavior of its COs. It is easy to find articles about COs being fired for personal misconduct, but it is difficult to find credible instances of the Navy covering up such behavior. Meanwhile, strict new requirements for screening potential commanders, such as written tests, oral boards, and even reviews from peers and subordinates, are being enacted throughout the Fleet.[5] Clearly, the Navy is willing to fight to preserve the standards to which it holds its COs.

Yet righting this ship will require more than emergency responses. First, the Navy should consider a new perspective on the meaning of integrity as it pertains to behavior, distinct from ethics and morality. Second, junior officers must cultivate a sense of individual responsibility for maintaining the highest standard of personal integrity. Otherwise, the Navy is at risk of sacrificing its long sacred standard of command performance, sinking into mediocrity and, eventually, failure.

Gaps in Character

When the alarm for General Quarters is sounded on U.S. Navy ships, the crew immediately shuts certain hatches, valves, and vents for maximum airtight and watertight integrity in the event of emergency. Today, the Navy must take similar action when it comes to personal integrity. Achieving physical integrity in a ship involves the elimination of gaps that would allow the intrusion and spread of dangers like seawater or fire. Personal integrity involves the elimination of inconsistencies between stated principles and behavior. These inconsistencies can be viewed as gaps in a leader's character. For COs who were relieved for personal misconduct, those gaps allowed corrosive agents such as mistrust or poor judgment to spread, eventually leading to the downfall of their careers.

It is a common misconception that "integrity" can be used interchangeably with words like "morality." Immorality can certainly account for the more egregious incidents, but is not as easily ascribed to behavior like drunk driving ("Prowler training squadron CO fired after DUI"), even though it is a clear violation of the Uniform Code of Military Justice (UCMJ).[6] Morality has some connotation of "goodness of character." Going back to its Latin root "integer" (whole, complete), integrity involves "consistency of character." Put simply, integrity is about doing what one says he or she is going to do. Officers agree not to drive drunk, so when COs get DUIs, they must be fired because they have shown a lack of integrity. Some philosophers argue that even morally reprehensible people, such as those involved in organized crime, can be said to have integrity because they live by the principles they espouse.

Why then should a virtue that can be associated with murderers and thieves be the focus of the Navy's effort to solve its personal-misconduct problems among COs? The key is that integrity provides the link between individual behavior and organizational principles, of which the Navy's are already beyond reproach. Several documents, including the Navy's Core Values Charter, the UCMJ, the Sailor's Creed, and the Oath of Office, lay out an unparalleled personal standard of conduct. For all intents and purposes, these documents represent a naval officer's "word" even if he or she has never explicitly expressed the Navy's principles. Simply by wearing the uniform, naval officers agree to abide by the standards and principles laid out before them. Yet, for all the Navy's morally upright principles, problems still persist. Clearly, there is a disconnect between certain COs' words and their actions, providing a textbook definition for a lack of integrity.

COs relieved because of personal misconduct did not necessarily lie, but integrity involves more than honesty. Like valves aligned on a ship, it involves aligning individual behavior with personal values and principles. These COs were not tasked with defining the Navy's principles, only embracing them. Furthermore, the situations that led to their downfall were not intense moral or ethical dilemmas. Questions of morality and ethics are often intractable, yet naval officers are expected to wrestle with and ultimately handle these issues. The aftermath of a true moral dilemma may not call a leader's integrity into question because there was no obvious "right" decision. There is, however, no moral dilemma involved in insulting, striking, and pouring beer on one's subordinates ("Report: Commander drunk, abusive in Bahrain").[7] There is only a lack of integrity.

An Individual Responsibility

Although the Navy's principles are dictated to commanding officers, it is not sufficient or even desired for them to just do what they are told. After all, a globally dispersed force depends on command initiative, and furthermore, COs are entrusted to make tough decisions that cannot be outlined in a set of rules. COs can look to the Navy's principles for guidance, but ultimately their integrity is determined by their making decisions that coincide with personally held values. Integrity is an inherently individual responsibility. All officers, regardless of command aspirations, must internalize the Navy's principles and take them aboard as their own. From early in their careers, officers should consciously examine any personal objections to the standard of conduct dictated by the Navy. Continuous integrity training should focus on studying the documents that prescribe values, principles, or personal behavior to officers, and taking action to resolve internal conflicts when necessary. For example, if an officer cannot agree with the Navy standard on behavior with the opposite sex, then he or she should petition to change the standard or resign.

Conversely, the Navy should be careful to keep the list of such documents as short as possible in recognition of the extreme personal commitment it requires of each officer. The service must also be cognizant of the standard set by the American people, whose expectations are not directly under the Navy's control. The public may perceive officers as lacking integrity because they failed to meet their expectations, even if none of the Navy's principles was violated. It is incumbent on the Navy to manage these expectations while each and every officer should strive to live up to them. As Army General John Vessey Jr. put it in his remarks to the 1983 graduating class of the Naval War College, "Inseparable from the concept of service is the concept of integrity. The citizens of this great nation place great trust in their military services. They will continue to judge us by stricter rules than they apply to themselves. And they should do that because, ultimately, their security rests with us and the way we perform our duties."[8]

The American people will not hold junior officers to a lower standard of integrity than COs, and neither should the Navy. To attack the root of integrity problems, officers must commit to the same high standard of integrity throughout their careers. Instead of testing integrity among potential COs and then relying on them to instill integrity among their subordinates, the effort should be focused directly at the most junior levels. In fact, the effort to cultivate integrity in officers must begin on Day One at the U.S. Naval Academy and all other commissioning programs.

Although COs sometimes seem to "flip a switch" when they exhibit behavior inconsistent with the Navy's principles, underlying integrity issues may have grown over time. Much like the slow spread of rust on a ship weakens its ability to withstand pressure, eventually causing structural failure, an officer without a well-developed sense of integrity will buckle under the burden and authority of command. Even a promising young officer may forget that respect for one's shipmates is a central Navy principle that he or she has sworn to uphold ("Cruiser CO relieved for 'cruelty'").[9]

A recent spate of integrity violations at the Naval Academy indicates that issues arise very early in an officer's career, and that the rash of CO firings may be only a symptom of a much wider epidemic. In 2009, the Academy had more integrity violations than it did in the previous 25 years (records on honor-code violations prior to 1984 are not available), with 140 substantiated and 21 midshipmen being sent home.[10] These numbers alone are not necessarily cause for concern. In fact, contrary to the trend of COs being relieved due to personal misconduct, these numbers may be a positive sign the Navy is getting serious about integrity. One would hope that most integrity violations occur at the beginning of an officer's career, rather than in a position of such great responsibility as command.

Building integrity involves education, not just discipline. Each year, midshipmen receive 12 hours of instruction on the Honor Concept (which begins "Midshipmen are persons of integrity.").[11] It is disturbing, however, that young officers appear to unlearn these lessons of honor and integrity as they go out into the Fleet. For example, midshipmen in all commissioning programs swear to abide by an Honor Code that is usually some form of "A midshipman does not lie, cheat, or steal." When they commission as ensigns, they are no longer held to such a strict standard. While the Honor Code does not cover every aspect of integrity, and arguably the Navy's Core Values or the UCMJ provide a similar standard of behavior, is there any reason to back away from such an explicit statement? The Honor Concept, or a version of the Honor Code, should be extended to apply to all commissioned officers.

Some midshipmen apparently believe that commissioned officers are granted more leeway on issues of honor and integrity. In 1995, when many of today's COs were commissioned, the Government Accountability Office released a report on service-academy honor and conduct systems. The report stated that 46 percent of Naval Academy midshipmen believe that "the concept of honor is much more stringent at the Academy than it is among active duty officers." In addition, midshipmen's views toward honor tended to become more negative as they progressed through the Academy. First-class midshipmen (seniors) saw more inconsistency than plebes (freshmen) in the application of the Honor Concept and saw fewer scenarios as integrity or honor violations.[12] These perceptions likely continue into an officer's commissioned service. This trend can be reversed if junior officers commit themselves to the same high standard of integrity to which the Navy is now holding its COs. Furthermore, the Navy should not consider rank when disciplining officers for integrity violations. The punishment (i.e., removal from current assignment) should be the same, although the ramifications would be more severe for more senior officers.

The Standard of Command Performance

While officers need more than integrity to succeed in command, without it they are destined to fail because there will be a lack of trust from their subordinates, peers, and superiors. A vigilant devotion to integrity builds trust, while one lapse can destroy it. "The Charge of Command," a 2011 memorandum sent to all prospective COs, states that "trust is a fundamental building block of our command and control structure and our ability to achieve mission success."[13] Given the importance the Navy places on trust in COs, it is easy to see why those displaying a lack of integrity are so readily fired. In fact, some argue that the Navy is paying more attention to integrity and therefore tolerating fewer personal shortcomings among its COs. This may be true, but getting rid of COs who behave badly only mitigates the problem. If it were a solution, then one would expect a decline in the rate of integrity violations among COs. Naval officers cannot afford to wait for that decline to appear.

Attitudes in the media suggest that COs, who are supposed to lead by example, are actually reinforcing the stereotype that the Navy has tried desperately to shake ("Like Drunken Sailors").[14] Some recent commentators even argue that the Navy has never held its COs to the same standard of personal integrity as command performance. Retired Rear Admiral Hamlin Tallent offers, "The Navy's acceptance of certain behavior is a lot more strict . . . it used to be widespread that guys were cheating on wives. Guys were fairly open about it."[15] Whether the change has been fueled by gender integration, sailors with smartphones and social media, or even a moral imperative, the Navy clearly understands it cannot enforce a double standard for COs. The standard of integrity must be commensurate with the standard of command performance, otherwise both will suffer, and the barrage of embarrassing headlines will continue to erode the trust the American people place in the Navy to accomplish its mission.

The standard of command performance is among the highest of any organization in the world and, to the Navy, it is sacred. As then–Captain James Stavridis wrote (with retired Vice Admiral William Mack) in *Command at Sea*, "In the U.S. Navy in particular, strict accountability is an integral part of command. Not even the profession of medicine embraces the absolute accountability found at sea. A doctor may lose a patient under trying circumstances and continue to practice, a naval officer seldom has the opportunity to hazard a second ship."[16]

It is important to note that a failure of performance is not the same as a failure of integrity, although the nature of command dictates that the Navy hold COs accountable for both. A CO should not be accused of lacking integrity because he runs his ship into a buoy, even if he is relieved of command. In 1983 General Vessey warned young naval officers not to confuse integrity with fallibility: "The warrior class has room for fallibility . . . there is no room for a lack of integrity."[17] Today, the Navy is sending a similar message to its COs by holding them to the same high standard of professional and personal accountability.

For now, at least, the Navy stands strong in holding COs accountable for their actions ("US Navy commander jailed for three years after pleading guilty to rape of two female sailors"), but it must guard against a "can't happen here" mentality.[18] Less egregious, yet still questionable, behavior has been tolerated by the chain of command ("40 faulted in *Enterprise* video investigation"), until it received national media attention.[19] It will take sustained commitment from individual officers to stop the flood of personal misconduct that threatens the Navy's foundational principles and standards.

Words and Actions

I do not claim to understand the burdens of command but, as Captain Harley Cope wrote in the preface to the first edition of *Command at Sea*, "Every young sailor who is worth his salt looks forward eagerly to his first command."[20] As a young naval officer, I have committed myself and my family to a life of service in hopes of achieving such a position. In looking forward, I know that I can succeed only if my sense of integrity is well developed long before (if ever) I take command of a ship. I believe there are other junior officers like me who are alarmed by the headlines they read but have not voiced their opinions. Who can blame them? What if their views on integrity are not consistent with that of senior leadership? What if they bring undue attention to the current situation by blowing it out of proportion? What if they become an example of a lack of integrity because of one mistake?

These are difficult questions that cannot be answered without taking action. It is my hope, however, that junior officers throughout the Fleet will bond together and start shutting these gaps in character by aligning their words with their actions. The Navy has established a watertight standard for personal integrity among its COs. It is up to future generations to either sink into failure, or rise to the challenge.

Lieutenant Drennan is a surface warfare officer. He recently completed an assignment as a Director Fellow in the Chief of Naval Operations' Strategic Studies Group and is now in department-head training at the Surface Warfare Officer School.

Notes

1. "Integrity: The Heart of Navy Core Values for the Submariner," www.navy .mil/navydata/cno/n87/usw/issue_9/integrity.html.

2. VADM Thomas Kilcline, "Developing the Whole Sailor," U.S. Naval Institute *Proceedings*, July 2010, http://www.usni.org/magazines/proceedings/2010 -07/developing-whole-sailor.

3. CAPT Mark Light, "The Navy's Moral Compass: Commanding Officers and Personal Misconduct," *Naval War College Review* (Summer 2012): 136–152.

4. "Submarine commander sunk after allegedly faking death to end affair," Fox News, 13 August 2012, www.foxnews.com/us/2012/08/13/sub-commander -allegedly-fakes-death-to-end-affair-is-relieved-from-duty; M. Thompson, "Navy Skippers: The Gift that Keeps on Giving," *Time*, 14 August 2012, http:// nation.time.com/2012/08/14/navy-skippers-the-gift-that-keeps-on-giving/.

5. S. Fellman, "CNO's tough new rules for screening commanders," *Navy Times*, 18 June 2012, http://scoopdeck.navytimes.com/2012/06/12/the -cnos-tough-new-rules-for-screening-skippers/.

6. G. Fuentes, "Prowler training squadron CO fired after DUI," *Navy Times*, 12 April 2011, www.navytimes.com/news/2011/04/navy-co-fired-prowler -squadron-dui-041211w.

7. B. Vergakis, "Report: Commander drunk, abusive in Bahrain," *Navy Times*, 7 October 2011, www.navytimes.com/news/2011/10/ap-commander-drunk -abusive-in-bahrain-100711/.

8. GEN John Vessey Jr., USA, "Remarks to the Graduating Class of the Naval War College," Newport, R.I., 24 June 1983.

9. P. Ewing, "Cruiser CO relieved for 'cruelty,'" *Navy Times*, 15 January 2010, www.navytimes.com/news/2010/01/ap_cowpens_cofired_011310/.

10. J. Murray, "What is the USNA Honor Concept?" *USNA or Bust!*, 26 March 2010, http://usnaorbust.wordpress.com/2010/03/26/what-is-the-usna-honor -code/.

11. M. Gebicke, "DOD Service Academies: Comparison of Honor and Conduct Adjudicatory Processes" (Washington, D.C.: United States General Account- ing Office, 1995).

12. Ibid.

13. ADM Gary Roughead, USN, "The Charge of Command," 9 June 2011.

14. S. W. Matthews, "Like Drunken Sailors," *The Daily*, 15 August 2012.

15. Ibid.

16. CAPT James Stavridis, USN, and VADM William Mack, USN (Ret.), *Command at Sea*, 5th ed. (Annapolis, Md.: Naval Institute Press, 1999).

17. Vessey, "Remarks to the Graduating Class."

18. J. Satherley, "US Navy commander jailed for three years after pleading guilty to rape of two female sailors," *Daily Mail*, 29 October 2011, www.dailymail .co.uk/news/article-2054986/US-Navy-commander-Jay-Wylie-jailed -pleading-guilty-rape-2-female-sailors.html.

19. W. H. McMichael, "40 faulted in Enterprise video investigation," *Navy Times*, 3 March 2011.

20. Stavridis and Mack, *Command at Sea*.

9 "MILITARY VIRTUE & THE FUTURE OF THE NAVAL SERVICE"

CAPT Michael Dunaway, USN

In a blunt and straightforward essay, the author recounts his relief from command of a guided-missile frigate as an illustration of what standards an officer is expected to uphold by the military and by the society it serves. He argues that if there is confusion, lack of clarity, absence of discussion of leadership and institutional standards within the services then erosion of the military ethos begins, with potentially devastating consequences for the individual leader, the service, and the nation.

"MILITARY VIRTUE & THE FUTURE OF THE NAVAL SERVICE"

By CAPT Michael Dunaway, USN, U.S. Naval Institute *Proceedings* (December 1998): 76–79.

The Navy must steer its course not by the stars, but by its principles.

There is a long and colorful literature, beginning at least with Homer, describing the values military forces and military personnel are believed to exemplify for society. These traits once were commonly referred to as "martial values" and included such characteristics as boldness, integrity, honor, courage, commitment, and intrepidity. Every civil society demands that its military personnel embrace values such as these and regards those who cannot as unworthy to wear their nation's uniform.

Martial values such as these define a military service as an institution—that is, an organization that embodies values a society considers indispensable. While society expects its military services to guard the nation's security, it also demands that its military institutions preserve those values for the good of the society. The fee society pays in return for this work of guardianship is to hold the institution in esteem and to honor its members.

One of the most famous American statements on this subject, William James's 1910 essay "The Moral Equivalent of War," asserts that a society devoid of military virtues such as "intrepidity, contempt of softness, surrender of private interest, . . . discipline and honor" would be hardly worth belonging to. In James's view, society has continual need for a living example of virtuous civic life, and those qualities exist nowhere else with such vitality as is found in the military. This need is one aspect of military service and military institutions that makes them indispensable to modern societies, and explains why even the most vocal critics of the U.S. military continue to insist that the services be held to a higher standard than society at large.

The difficulty, however, lies in determining exactly what that standard should be. The values that society holds in esteem (and that the military is expected to preserve) change as society's needs change. The fundamental question is: Which values are enduring and must be respected and cultivated, and which are transient or faddish and should be resisted?

This problem is the central cultural issue with which American society and the military services currently are grappling. Specifically, is military virtue the same for a fully integrated, all-volunteer military in peacetime as for America's earlier conscripted militaries during wartime? Are they the same virtues for a military whose nation sends it to do nonmilitary missions? Can military virtue be corrupted by the integration of women; by our reliance on technology; by jointness?

If William James was correct—that a society devoid of military virtue is on its way to becoming unworthy of any ideals whatsoever—where should society look for an example of military virtue if not to the military services themselves?

Judging from recent newspaper headlines, the U.S. military is seeing troubled times. Popular analysis of these problems has focused largely on the services' difficulties in incorporating women into the fighting forces.

While this may contain an element of truth, the problem more accurately resides in confusion within the services themselves about which principles the military institution is to be guided by, and the suspicion among senior officers that frank discussion about principles is frivolous at best and a disloyal airing of dirty linen at worst.

However, even though our understanding of military virtue may appear directly relevant to the integrity of the military services as institutions, it inevitably affects the integrity and effectiveness of the fighting forces themselves and the way they are operated.

By way of illustrating the consequences of our current state, I offer two examples: an incident that resulted in my relief from command, and the death of Admiral Boorda.

Moral Authority and Command Autonomy

In the middle of my tour as commanding officer of a guided-missile frigate, I was relieved of command for initiating a man overboard drill by jumping over the side while the ship was transiting between battle-group exercises in the Caribbean Sea. As you might imagine, this is a pretty good sea story, though not germane in every detail to the subject at hand. Suffice it to say that the exercise had nothing to do with assessing the crew's ability to recover a man in the water (which they had demonstrated on numerous occasions), but everything to do with my crew's recovery of a long dormant faith in their own abilities—a faith I wanted them to know I had, and which their subsequent actions affirmed.

What is germane to the current question is the series of events that followed. After completing the battle-group exercises and two more weeks of

Caribbean operations, we returned to home port where—a month after the incident—the commodore of my parent squadron relieved me of command and then directed an investigation into the incident. During the succeeding months I initiated a series of letters to various echelons within the administrative chain of command, culminating in a request for review of the case by the Board for Correction of Naval Records (BCNR). In my submission to BCNR, I requested that its determination be forwarded to the Chief of Naval Operations (CNO) for information in the event that my detachment from command was upheld. The Board declined to honor that request, citing governing instructions, but stated that it would be permissible to write the CNO directly. This I eventually did; excerpts appear on these pages.

There are two reasons why I offer this firsthand account of a bit of recent naval history. The first deals with our collective reaction to Admiral Boorda's death and how I believe we should endeavor to understand it. The second reason is more directly related to the subject of this article—the definition of military virtue in the current political context, and the centrality of ethical and forthright leadership to the future of the U.S. Navy.

As former Secretary of the Navy John Lehman pointed out, the death of a serving Chief of Naval Operations is a question of national magnitude. No one is likely to shed enough light on that tragedy to explain it to the satisfaction of the members of the naval service or to the nation. And yet, we share a collective responsibility to attempt to understand that event in order that, where changes can be made for the good of the service, they are made.

It may be true that one specific event (Admiral Boorda's condemnation of himself for wearing unearned combat devices) may have served as the catalyst for the CNO's decision to end his own life. But the larger reason was almost certainly an accumulation of internal conflicts that he faced in having to reconcile the equally compelling demands of competing value systems.

For example, his decision not to act on my request—that the circumstances of my relief from command be made known to the naval surface force—seemed out of character with his customary style of leadership. The statement in his CNO Weekly Update emphasizing the importance of communications "at a time when communication is vital, when our people want and deserve to hear from their leadership" made his failure to follow his own good advice all the more difficult to comprehend.

Certainly, his distinction as the first commander to authorize the offensive use of force by NATO (in Bosnia, 1994) made his explanation of my failure to consider what "might have happened" on board my own ship seem inconsistent. Nevertheless, as Admiral Boorda himself wrote, without real information, "there are enough conflicting stories about important events that one can get just about any version possible, even remotely possible."

However, there is a much more important reason for the Navy's coming to terms with Admiral Boorda's death. Without a reasoned dialogue about its causes and its consequences, we risk learning the wrong lessons from that tragedy. A frequently heard explanation was that Admiral Boorda was the most visible (though not the first) casualty in a cultural war between the Navy and political factions within our own society. Like all wars, a cultural war presumes the existence of enemies. In this case, however, those enemies would be fellow U.S. citizens in positions of influence and authority within the federal government.

Political adversaries notwithstanding, the underlying and dangerous logic of this explanation is twofold. First, it implies that the Navy's leadership lacks the authority or the intellectual stamina to defend itself and the service against such enemies. Second, it assumes that the institution of the Navy can be negatively influenced by external forces to a greater degree than it can be positively shaped by the leadership within it. Either one of these alternatives clears the way for the leadership's abdication of responsibility for formulating the service's policies and defending its principles.

Leadership and Institutional Standards

This leads to the second reason why I offer this brief sea story: the role of leadership in defining the standards of the institution.

In a March 1995 article entitled "On American Principles," George Kennan differentiated between the role of policy and that of principle in the shaping of a nation or its institutions. Chief among them is that a policy requires rational justification in order for it to make any sense. A principle, on the other hand, is guided by the dictates of conscience and a commitment to a specific self-identity, and does not necessarily require any explanation at all.

The phrase "a matter of principle" indicates the existence of a boundary beyond which an individual, an institution, or a nation simply will not go, whereas a policy is a specific rule operating within the broader confines of those principles. Most importantly, the task of defining principles "must be seen as not just a privilege, but also a duty of . . . leadership."

My experience indicated a considerable lack of clarity within our institution regarding the roles of policy and principle. As I wrote to Admiral Boorda, no officer in my chain of command ever provided an explanation about the nature of my error while I was in command. The CNO's own statement that "we don't need a written rule which says that commanders shouldn't expose themselves to needless danger" begs the question of how that particular policy is to be taken in light of my own experience. Do the consequences of my actions now constitute an unwritten rule for all COs? What degree of authority should be attributed to an "unwritten rule," and how is it to be promulgated and administered? How does that rule relate to the CNO's statement concerning "unnecessary risks," and "objective measures"—which by tradition, if not by actual regulation, have been the specific authority of the operational commander on scene rather than of the administrative chain of command back in home port?

Regarding the role of principle in operational decision-making, one publication of the naval service, Fleet Marine Force Manual One (FMFM-1) *Warfighting*, offers an unambiguous statement regarding the relationship between risk and leadership:

> Boldness is an essential moral trait in a leader, for it generates combat power beyond the physical means at hand. Initiative, the willingness to act on one's own judgment, is a prerequisite for boldness. These traits carried to excess can lead to rashness, but we must realize that

errors by junior leaders stemming from overboldness are a necessary part of learning. We should deal with such errors leniently; there must be no "zero defects" mentality. Not only must we not stifle boldness or initiative, we must continue to encourage both traits *in spite of mistakes.* [Emphasis in original.]

This is a statement that transcends military doctrine and could stand as a principle for a life successfully and honestly lived. Whether it constitutes a military virtue that only the Marine Corps is willing to honor in the current political climate is something that the Navy's senior leaders will have to decide. I would offer, however, that a military force that will not tolerate a certain sort of audacity in its day-to-day routines is likely to find audacity lacking when it counts. As we continually tell ourselves, we fight the way we train. Most certainly, we fight the way we *think.* The alternative is to accept the form of institutional behavior said to have been inculcated in members of the British Foreign Service in the years leading up to World War I: "Actions have consequences; consequences are unpredictable; therefore, take no action."

Policy, Principle, and Precedent

This leads to a final point concerning the issue of precedent. Precedent has an unpleasant way of filling the vacuum left in the absence of either policy or principle. The fundamental question is how the experiences related above are to be understood by officers now aspiring to command. If COs are trained—indeed, compelled—to think first of their own safety and of the viability of their careers, that is surely what they will do.

However, a more worthy precedent for this institution was established in 1779 with our Navy's first engagement between the *Serapis* and the *Bonhomme Richard*—notable among other reasons for the fact that John Paul Jones was not summarily relieved of command afterward because he *might* have lost.

If any lesson is to be learned from the suicide of a Chief of Naval Operations, it should be that good men find their lives unworthy when they are unable to reconcile their principles with those they believe are forced upon them by circumstances or by a perceived responsibility to maintaining the appearance of infallibility. The same thing can be said of a nation's attitude toward its institutions.

Our failure to honor principles by which we have defined ourselves for more than 200 years—or to establish the extent of the currently acceptable boundaries through a process of corporal punishment promulgated via sanctioned rumor—is an invitation to institutional disaster.

Our responsibility for defining the nature of the military ethos in the modern profession of arms and what that ethos contributes to society can neither be ignored nor delegated. The day we warriors stop endeavoring to clarify our principles and apply them in day-to-day operations is the day we cease being an American institution and become merely a band of technically proficient mercenaries. The American people recognize this—and it forms the basis of their confidence in us as surely as our expertise at warfighting.

For this reason it is not enough that we settle for "the best damn Navy in the world." The nation needs that, certainly; but it also needs a naval service worthy of the nation's unqualified trust and confidence. What we need is not a warfighting revival, but a revival of military virtue: an understanding of where we stand, what principles we stand for, and a resolute refusal to yield to political expediencies—real or perceived. Anything less would be a disservice to our nation and a betrayal of the best that the history and traditions of the Navy represent. It all depends on the principles by which we steer our course.

Captain Dunaway, a 1973 graduate of the U.S. Naval Academy, serves on the faculty of the National War College.

10 "READINESS IS A MORAL RESPONSIBILITY"

BG D. L. Grange, USA (Ret.)

Professional military ethics entails much more than a checklist of dos and don'ts. Brigadier General Grange contends that if a unit is not operationally ready for a mission then there are ethical as well as operational shortcomings in command leadership. His thoughtful piece opens the aperture on what is and is not within the domain of ethics and encourages leaders to have a holistic rather than a fragmented or compartmentalized understanding of leadership and command.

"READINESS IS A MORAL RESPONSIBILITY"

By BG D. L. Grange, USA (Ret.), U.S. Naval Institute *Proceedings* (April 2000): 2.

> *American soldiers have always had the will to win. What they need are commanders willing to prepare—and prepared to do what must be done for readiness. The required tenacity to make things happen is a commander's responsibility.*

The first priority for a leader is unit readiness. Despite shortfalls of people, funding, and equipment; high operational tempo; short turnarounds; the erosion

71

of benefits (or at least that perception); and an antiquated readiness assessment and reporting system—Americans expect their military to achieve unequivocal success on any assigned mission. You have to be ready to go.

Providing the resources, training, and mental preparation for units and soldiers is a commander's first quality-of-life responsibility. It must become an organization's way of life if soldiers are to be capable of transitioning to combat immediately from peacekeeping, humanitarian assistance, or other non-combat missions. Maintaining a constant combat capability will give the unit the required baseline to function throughout today's increasingly uncertain and complex spectrum of conflict. Well-trained, disciplined soldiers in a combat-focused unit can adapt quickly, but they should never be asked to do something for which they have not trained.

Soldiers expect a commander to make a difference. They want to be part of a well-trained unit, and the key to this is trained, confident commanders—and command is neither a "check-the-block" sequence nor a position of entitlement. It is a cherished privilege, an honor, and one should fight to stay in command as long as possible. The common one-year company-command tours do not allow time to develop a future battalion commander. Such short tours do not provide a commander the time to understand fully the combination of the elements of combat power and the judgment necessary on the field of battle.

Affording subordinate commanders the opportunity to master the elements of combat power—maneuver, firepower, protecting the force, and, most important, the integrating element of leadership—requires an extraordinary commitment of time and effort by the chain of command. Prescriptive training may suffice for tactics, techniques, procedures, and drills, but a commander must take junior leaders beyond the mechanical, material multipliers of combat power and teach the importance of the intangible and non-material factors of readiness. Junior leaders must be trained to think and operate in uncertain, ambiguous environments. Only then can they be expected to cope with the unforeseen.

People are more important than hardware, but there must be a balance. Since the soldier is the strongest and weakest part of any system, developing the human dimension must come first. Developing true esprit de corps is much

more than just blurting out catch phrases when you salut(
look in the eye of each soldier, the pride in the unit, the
the compassion for comrades in arms, and the desire to
must be shown what "right" looks like with realistic trai
comes from understanding what it takes to execute successfully a unit's critical
tasks and what is expected of individual soldiers.

Using personal experience, mentorship from seasoned field leaders, and
healthy cross-talk between commanders of the combined arms team, leaders
must assess their organization's state of readiness, develop an appropriate training plan, and find the necessary resources. Shortages inevitably will exist, but
such challenges are not new; good commanders solve them.

The moral responsibility for readiness requires a commander to go after
the resources to generate training miles in the field, both internally and through
the chain of command. Appropriate simulations can be used, but they must be
balanced by field training, where soldiers can smell the smoke, hear the noise,
feel the shock, see the results, understand the danger, and experience the excite-
ment. Commanders must ensure there is sufficient ammunition for soldier
turnover on individual weapons, crew continuity, and combined-arms live-fire
maneuver. They must keep the pressure on the system to field equipment shortfalls, find parts, use contract maintenance to solve critical personnel shortfalls,
and implement practical cost-saving maintenance procedures. They must inno-
vate to increase realism, and stand firm if challenged by higher headquarters
when conducting other than prescribed, set-piece training.

Most important, a commander must go after people. Leaders should not
accept anything but required strength; military organizations were designed to
fight at required strength, not at a reduced authorization. There is no slop built
into a military organization. Even at 100% of required fill, a unit will be unable
to ship out much beyond 90% because of the inevitable non-deployables. Leaders must balance the demands for post support and other tasks that strip their
ranks of field strength necessary to conduct first-rate training. A commander
must set priorities ruthlessly, constantly challenging piecemeal requirements
from higher headquarters.

ou will go to war the way you are today, not the way you hope to be. Senior
aders who place extraordinary pressure on junior commanders to accomplish
a myriad of tasks with zero casualties and mistakes, without providing them
sufficient resources, have failed in their moral obligation for readiness.

Juma Ikanga, winner of the New York City marathon, summed it up elo-
quently: "The will to win is not nearly as important as the will to prepare."
American soldiers have always had the will to win. What they need are com-
manders willing to prepare—and prepared to do what must be done for readiness.
The required tenacity to make things happen is a commander's responsibility.
Total commitment is a tall order, and there is no substitute for strong leadership.
That leadership requires moral courage of the highest order.

Brigadier General Grange, U.S. Army (Retired), Special Forces and
Infantry, commanded the 1st Infantry Division prior to his retirement.

11 "THE CHALLENGE OF MORAL LEADERSHIP"

CAPT Michael J. O'Hara, USMC

Awarded First Honorable Mention in the Vincent Astor Memorial Leadership Essay Contest in 1977, this article draws upon foundational documents of the profession of arms, philosophy, history, and literature to study moral aspects of leadership. The author links morality with responsibility with respect to leadership and argues that both are basic and essential components that must be attained and maintained by the naval leader.

"THE CHALLENGE OF MORAL LEADERSHIP"

By CAPT Michael J. O'Hara, USMC, U.S. Naval Institute *Proceedings* (August 1977): 58–62.

Vincent Astor Memorial Leadership Contest,
First Honorable Mention

A few years ago a group of experts met in Washington to discuss the question, "Can America survive the next war?" They were concerned primarily with whether a large, industrialized, technologically dependent nation could recover from the damage which would ensue from a major nuclear attack. Although their conclusions were guardedly optimistic, they limited discussion to physical survival and virtually ignored the less visible, but no less important, damage that would be done to the spiritual fabric of society. This is not surprising since ours is a society which is much more comfortable with analysis and measurement than it is with such abstract and frustratingly imprecise concepts as duty, responsibility, and morality.

As the naval service becomes increasingly dependent on technology, its officers may well be increasingly tempted to give in to that same tendency to judge success in terms of systems efficiency—the managerial dimension—rather than in terms of personal values. The inclination to do so already exists. Inspections at all levels of command regularly zero in on the measurable. "People programs" notwithstanding, such criteria as reporting error rates, equipment readiness statistics, and stock inventory levels often become the index by which an officer's fitness for command is evaluated. No doubt these criteria are vitally important within the context of any complex organization, but the danger arises when the system is emphasized at the expense of the men and women who make it work.

Without getting into the "leader" *vs.* "manager" debate, I believe it is fair to state that although the leader and manager both must concern themselves with systems efficiency and organizational effectiveness, the manager regards people primarily as a factor in the equation of goal attainment while the leader must regard them as ends in themselves. In fact, this latter approach lies at the very foundation of traditional military leadership.

The responsibilities of leadership are perhaps greater today than they ever have been in the past. In addition to mastering vast quantities of information, the modern leader must be prepared to deal with a better educated, more articulate subordinate who is often skeptical of authority. The responsibilities, however, remain the same, though some are less difficult than others because their effects are measurable. To ensure that subordinates are adequately fed, clothed, and berthed is relatively simple because the results are apparent. Knowledge can be tested, and performance evaluated. However, the leader's responsibility for the moral welfare of his men is altogether more difficult because its results are intangible and hinge directly on what he is, not on what he knows or says. To project the proper image is the most fundamental and challenging of a leader's responsibilities.

U.S. Navy Regulations, under "Requirement for Exemplary Conduct," states:

> All commanding officers and others in authority in the naval service are required to show in themselves a good example of virtue, honor, patriotism and subordination; to be vigilant in inspecting the conduct of all persons who are placed under their command; to guard against and suppress all dissolute and immoral practices, and to correct, according to the laws and regulations of the Navy, all persons who are guilty of them; and to take all necessary and proper measures, under the laws, regulations and customs of the naval service, to promote and safeguard the morale, the physical well-being, and the general welfare of the officers and enlisted persons under their command or charge. (10 USC 5947)

It is significant that this requirement is placed not on the inspector general, the chaplain, or the senior enlisted man, but on the commanding officer or others in authority. Yet sometimes, it seems, the requirement is not met, and there is a reason why.

The moral revolution, which has taken place throughout the world during the past 15 years, has challenged some of the basic tenets of Judeo-Christian ethics. Values once held so sacred as to be unquestionable have been freely and publicly scorned to the point where even those with a strongly developed moral sense have felt the stirrings of self-doubt. The process has not been entirely bad, however. Values which are adhered to through the influence of tradition are bound to be weaker and less effective than those which are held as the result of experience and reflection. So the attacks on traditional ethics have served a useful purpose in that they have forced people to reexamine their moral premises and reevaluate their beliefs. But this is an essentially negative reaction to a problem which deserves a more positive approach. It is too easy to slip into a "fortress mentality" and insist that what is traditional is right because it is traditional. Socrates laid down the first principle of philosophy when he said, "The unexamined life is not worth living," and perhaps it is the most traditional, the most dearly held beliefs that need to be examined first, then reaffirmed, modified, or even rejected if it is discovered that they have lost their currency. This seems to be what is happening in the world today. Certainly not all who question traditional values are moral anarchists. When men of good will can be found on both sides of such questions as homosexuality and abortion, to name only two of the more controversial, then something profoundly important is happening.

Whether the outcome of the struggle will be the triumph of traditionalism or some blending of traditional and modern ideas, it is impossible to say. But one effect of the struggle is already clear. As the tempo of the attack on established values has intensified, people in general, military officers among them, have become less sure of their moral premises and consequently more prone to tolerate violations of time-honored standards of moral behavior. Yet the requirement of exemplary conduct remains, clear and unequivocal. An officer in the naval service is required not only to set the example, but to create a healthy moral climate in which the men and women under his charge can develop their characters to the fullest. The role of the leader assumes even greater importance when we consider that the struggle between Communism and democracy is not merely a rivalry between two political and economic systems, but a conflict between two diametrically opposed views of the nature and worth of the human spirit. If we prevail, it will be due less to the potency of our armaments than to the strength of our spirit. This is the greatest challenge of moral leadership.

Law and regulation lay down our responsibilities in this area, but to carry them out intelligently and effectively, we must understand them. Basically there are two sources for our concept of morality: religion and philosophy (or ethics). The religious concept of morality is based on the premises that man has been created by God and placed on earth to aid in the fulfillment of a divine plan; that the trials of life are a test which, if passed, will merit eternal reward;

and that during the course of his life man is expected to observe certain moral precepts which will make him pleasing in the sight of God. Although God works through human nature and not against it, so that to be truly good is to be truly human, religious morality is still essentially authoritarian. Obedience to the divine will is the main requirement. Morality based on philosophy or ethics, on the other hand, takes man as its starting point and asks what is the nature of man and how must he act to be true to it. These questions have been asked and answered by philosophers from the time of man's first reflection on his condition. Although there has been a wide divergence of opinion over the ages, certain basic principles have been agreed upon:[1] (1) man has a nature—that is, there is something unique to man which distinguishes him from all other living and nonliving things; (2) man can know his nature—that is, he can recognize that he is something separate and apart from the rest of creation and that what differentiates him is his capacity for thought; (3) man can know that he should live and act in accordance with his nature—that is, he has a moral sense; and (4) man can live and act in accordance with his nature—that is, he has the ability to make right moral choices.

These four principles are the basis of that natural law which holds that "good" is that which advances man's nature; "evil" is that which retards it. Different philosophers at different times have challenged the theory, but it has been unusually persistent, mostly because it makes sense. To deny it requires the assumption either that man's nature is intrinsically evil and that "good" is therefore unnatural or anti-human, or that man has no nature, or if he has, he cannot know it. Both assumptions reduce the human condition to an absurdity. We treat plants differently than we do animals because we have learned from experience what it takes to raise each to its highest level of development. In other words, each has a nature and we know what it is. To say that we can know the lesser orders of existence, and yet not know ourselves, however imperfectly, is illogical and contradicted by experience.

Once we accept the theory, we are faced with the question of what constitutes the good which advances man's nature. There are many possible answers, but the best and simplest is that those things are good which allow a man to develop his potential as a man. Most answers to philosophical questions lead immediately to still more questions, and it is beyond the scope of this essay to deal with the question of what it means to be a man. It is enough to say that our form of government is based on the premise that man is a creature endowed with the inalienable rights of life, liberty, and the pursuit of happiness and that the purpose of government is to ensure that he has the opportunity to exercise those rights within a social context. Rights imply responsibilities, and since the context in which we operate is social, we exercise our rights and carry out our responsibilities with respect to others as well as ourselves. Responsibilities, of course, vary in degree. The responsibility of parent for child or teacher for student is greater than that of neighbor for neighbor. It hinges in large part on the extent to which one is dependent on the other. The dependence of the led on the leader is greater in the military service than in any other profession. Consequently the responsibility of the military leader is greater. Having sworn to defend the Constitution, he is required to do so not only in a purely military sense, but also by exemplifying and upholding the moral principles on which the Constitution is based. He is, in short, required to be a gentleman.

The word "gentleman" is not easy to define with any precision and perhaps no definition could do the concept full justice. The *Manual for Courts-Martial* defines it by its antithesis when it states, "There are certain moral attributes common to the ideal officer and the perfect gentleman, a lack of which is indicated by acts of dishonesty or unfair dealing, of indecency or indecorum, or of lawlessness, injustice, or cruelty." Fortunately we are not expected to be paragons of virtue, for as the article continues, "Not everyone is or can be expected to meet ideal moral standards, but there is a limit of tolerance below which the individual standards of an officer . . . cannot fall without seriously compromising his standing as an officer . . . or his character as a gentleman." This is not an abstract ideal to be pursued for its own sake, nor is it merely a reflection of the aristocratic origin of so many military traditions. It is a fundamental guide to practical, effective leadership.

To be effective, an officer must have character, which is simply the strength of will to do what is required when some other course of action might be more attractive. Character can be developed only through practice, through a long series of individual acts of the will, the end result of which is dependability. There is probably no more essential leadership trait. "An officer without character," as General S. L. A. Marshall wrote, "is more useless than a ship with no bottom."[2] To be effective an officer must inspire the respect of his subordinates, not only by his professional competence, but by his personal integrity as well. If he shows a weakness for alcohol or gambling or women, he will be perceived as weak in other areas and the respect he needs to lead will diminish accordingly. Finally, to be truly effective, an officer must set the example in such a way that he becomes a role-model for his subordinates. He will be one in any case, for good or ill. The standard he sets will be the one they emulate. But only if he demands the best of his men in behavior and conduct, by showing the way himself, will they be psychologically and morally prepared for the stress and danger they might someday face in war. The practical effect of good example is good discipline, a point well made in the following excerpt from the *Naval Officer's Guide:*[3] "*Good example* on the part of officers is one of the prime requisites to maintenance of good discipline. In fact, it is no exaggeration to say that the true, desirable brand of discipline can neither be instilled nor maintained unless the officers *practice what they preach*. Our men are too intelligent and too high-spirited to extend respect and loyalty to men of hypocrisy, insincerity, and sham."

Character, integrity, and good example are traits of a gentleman. A leader who does not possess them is, in fact, no leader at all whatever billet or rank he may hold. They are also moral qualities, practical in that the extent to which they are present in a command, among officers and men alike, stands in direct relation to the level of morale and respect for authority. In their absence, a unit will suffer not only a loss in morale, discipline, and efficiency, but also will be seriously compromised in its ability to carry out its mission. There can be no more practical reason for insisting that officers be gentlemen.

Moral leadership is difficult because, as stated earlier, it depends on what a man is. No amount of reading, study, or reflection will make an officer morally fit unless it is accompanied by a conscious, unremitting effort at self-improvement. Moral living is not passive. It is more than just not doing bad things. It is an active process of personal struggle against weakness, expediency, and self-doubt, and its rewards are strength of character, resolution, and confidence. The officer who is unwilling to make the effort himself has no right to demand it of his men.

Moral leadership is especially difficult today because modern society has slipped its ethical moorings. We live in an age of skepticism toward all traditional values, and even the churches no longer enjoy the respect they once had. It is not surprising, then, that many of the young people coming into the service today are resistant to authority and resent any attempt to modify their behavior in the direction of what they see as establishment norms. Much of the fault is ours. We have recruited them with promises of education, adventure, travel, and "fun," and it isn't until after they have committed themselves that they learn that duty is a hard, exacting taskmaster. Some of them feel cheated, or at least deceived, and so become more resistant. Perhaps that is the inevitable result of trying to sell service to country as if it were toothpaste. On the bright side, most young servicemen are as idealistic as they have ever been, although they often go to great lengths to hide it. Their skepticism is a kind of defense mechanism against what they regard as the hypocrisy of society. Fortunately, few of them are cynical. Cynicism seems to be a disease of age and experience. They can still be reached by officers who are willing to show them the way. Those who come from stable homes where they received strong moral guidance from their parents will expect the same from their officers. But those whose backgrounds have been unstable are in the greatest need of positive guidance. Though they won't admit it and may not even be consciously aware of it, they want it. Since human nature tends toward the good, an appeal to a man's best instincts usually will not fail.

Next to personal example, the most essential ingredient of successful moral leadership is a proper relationship between an officer and his subordinates. What that relationship should be was perhaps best expressed by Major General John A. Lejeune, 13th Commandant of the Marine Corps, when, in paragraph 5390.0 of the *Marine Corps Manual*, he wrote:

The relation between officers and enlisted men should in no sense be that of superior and inferior nor that of master and servant, but rather that of teacher and scholar. In fact, it should partake of the nature of the relation between father and son, to the extent that officers, especially commanders, are responsible for the physical, mental, and moral welfare, as well as the discipline and military training of the men under their command who are serving the Nation in the Marine Corps.

Although he should be the embodiment of personal virtue, an officer will be totally ineffective in his role as a moral leader if he projects an attitude of superiority. His men will be quick to sense and resent it. This is not to say that he must compromise his personal or professional standards or pretend to be less than he is. On the contrary, as a leader he is expected to be better than the men he leads. But as a moral man he will be acutely aware that character is formed not over days and weeks, but over years, and he will approach his task with the humility that comes from an appreciation of his own human weakness. And he will never forget that his goal is not to make saints of soldiers, but to develop disciplined fighting men who will stand up under the rigors of combat.

According to one of the popular clichés of the '60s, the military is a microcosm of society. The phrase was repeated so often that many came to believe it even though it is true only in a limited sense. Certainly young men and women do not shed their problems along with their civilian clothes when they arrive at boot camp or OCS, and if drug abuse and racial discrimination are problems in the civilian community, they will be problems in the military as well. But a military organization is in no sense simply a mirror-image of the society from which it draws its members. It is an institution with a unique set of values and a code of ethics all its own. Therein lies its strength. While attitudes toward moral issues within society at large periodically swing from conservative to liberal and back again, depending on the prevailing climate of opinion, the military remains constant in its adherence to traditional values. As an institution, the military is inherently conservative, in the root sense of the word; that is, its function is to conserve, as well as to defend, the principles on which the nation was founded. In many ways this makes it easier for the officer to carry out his moral leadership responsibilities. Working within a closed society, he is less subject to the winds of change blowing in the outside world. Along with his commission he has accepted a moral and ethical code which it becomes his duty to live by and inculcate in his subordinates. If he has a strong religious faith, then the support he will derive from it will be inestimable, but even if he lacks that kind of faith, the code will be his source of strength.

Much more could be said on the subject of moral leadership, particularly in the area of its practical application. Drug and alcohol abuse, racial discrimination, and financial irresponsibility are a few of the problems which demand the leader's attention in the day-to-day performance of his duties. The more general problems of conduct in time of war might also have been addressed. But I considered it more useful to reemphasize fundamentals. The leader who adopts them as the basis of his personal ethic usually will not have trouble applying them in any situation.

Morality is simply another word for responsibility—responsibility to oneself and to others, but it is not uniquely the concern of the leader. It is the concern of every man and woman who wants to be truly human. For the military leader, however, it assumes particular importance since his sole reason for being is to set the example for others, to show them the way, to *lead*. In the words of the poet Chaucer, "If gold ruste, what shal iren do?" For all its difficulties, the burden of moral leadership will be gladly borne by any officer who recognizes its significance. This is the challenge and the reward.

Notes

1. See Leo R. Ward, *Ethics: A College Text* (New York: Harper & Row, 1965), 142–143.
2. See S. L. A. Marshall, *The Officer as a Leader* (Harrisburg, Pa.: Stackpole, 1966).
3. See Arthur A. Ageton and William P. Mack, *The Naval Officer's Guide,* 8th ed. (Annapolis, Md.: United States Naval Institute, 1970).

12 "WORSE THAN A FAILURE OF LEADERSHIP"

CAPT Thomas B. Grassey, USNR (Ret.)

By any reasonable standard the prisoner abuses at Abu Ghraib prison in Iraq in 2003 were wrong. Ethics professor Thomas Grassey argues that to call what happened a "failure of leadership" is unwise, vague, and ignores potential systemic deficiencies in doctrine, training, and organizations. He also believes that it is quietly self-exonerating in that by using a vague phrase, we consciously or subconsciously think that it could not happen to us. To hold such a belief, he argues, is to underestimate the darker potentials of human nature under extreme circumstances and the ever-present potential of abusing one's power. Bad things *can* happen, but they need not happen and Grassey provides eight succinct reminders for leaders to help avoid another tragic episode like Abu Ghraib.

"WORSE THAN A FAILURE OF LEADERSHIP"

By CAPT Thomas B. Grassey, USNR (Ret.), U.S. Naval Institute *Proceedings* (December 2006): 44–47.

A professor of leadership and ethics at the Naval War College outlines the real reasons for prisoner abuse and lays out ways military leaders can keep such things from happening.

To describe the U.S. military's mistreatment of prisoners at Abu Ghraib, Guantanamo Bay, Bagram, and elsewhere as a failure of leadership is unwise. Yet this phrase is seemingly all that men and women in the U.S. armed forces are willing to admit should be learned from crimes that have done great harm to our nation and to everyone who does or will wear the uniform. Why are these actions worse than just failures of leadership?

First, such a characterization is vague. At what level or levels did leadership fail? Non-commissioned officers, company-grade, field-grade, general officers, and the highest-level civilian leaders of American forces have all been charged with leadership failures leading to abuses of prisoners. Who are we saying actually fell short? And if these behaviors were failures of leadership, why have so few (if any) leaders been held accountable?

Second, a failure of leadership supports the idea that a few bad apples, poorly led and inadequately supervised, were the exclusive cause of the problems. It ignores the possibility that systemic deficiencies in doctrine, training, regulations, and organization—as well as leadership itself—need to be identified and corrected.

Third, such a failure is immodestly but quietly self-exonerating. Since we can recognize the errors of others, we imagine that we are better leaders than they were, so we would not have made their mistakes. A reassuring thought, no doubt, but perhaps a mistaken one, and clearly one that precludes self-examination and genuine learning. "Couldn't happen to me" is probably false, and certainly dangerous.

So what should good leaders at all levels identify as reminders to be gleaned from the parade of abuses—including deaths from torture—enemy prisoners have suffered at the hands of uniformed U.S. personnel?

Good People Can Be Sadistic

Everything about the behaviors and psychologies of human beings applies full strength to those great Americans you lead. However well trained and highly motivated our all-volunteer forces are, they are still subject to the same stresses, temptations, vulnerabilities, and passions as all human beings. Understand those dangers and train to cope against them, but ensure that the chain of command is monitoring their inevitable assault on the behavior and character of your command so corrective action is quickly brought to bear.

As U.S. prisons and numerous academic studies (most famously by Stanley Milgram and Philip Zimbardo) show, situations where normal, good people are given power over others are fraught with dangers of inhumane, even sadistic, treatment. No officer should have been surprised that inadequately supervised guards fell prey to such temptation.

More generally, being an American offers no one an exemption from the passions of battle, the desire for vengeance, the lure of power, the urge to dehumanize, the temptation of sadism, and the traps of irrationality and brutality. No one is ever far from those evils, and an environment of life-and-death danger brings all of us face-to-face with those aspects of human nature.

Leadership Counts

The only bulwarks against these dark urges are self-control and external discipline. We know that, in the violence of war on a foreign land against members of an alien society using despicable tactics, the concept of "self" is readily overshadowed; individuals become part of a mass, a herd. Self-control recedes or disappears, and what too often governs is mass behavior.

The regulation of mass behavior is precisely what military discipline is designed to effect. In the most extreme earthly approximation of hell—marked by darkness, noise, fear, hatred, isolation, exhaustion, and sudden death—military discipline controls the behavior of the mass of men subjected to such terror. Similarly, it regulates the individual's conduct in less severe environments in which self-control by itself may not be sufficient to maintain minimal standards of behavior.

The ability of men and women under your authority to conduct themselves honorably in the stress of war depends on your leadership in infusing a sense of unit discipline. Whether it is a squad or a joint task force, your subordinates need your leadership, lest they fall prey to our common human weaknesses.

Thus, you can make a difference. But leadership isn't a position you have, it's simply what you do. Nothing counts but your actions. Your career history, technical expertise, command philosophy, professional wisdom, and good intentions all matter only to the extent they cause your behavior and produce desired specific actions by others.

Now, leaders are busy people, so they need to be clear about priorities. Focus your limited time and energy first on what is mission-critical. As far as your unit is concerned, that must always be priority one.

But don't forget priority two: Avoid fatal mistakes. Usually, there are many ways to accomplish the mission: some of these also entail disastrous methods that undermine long-run mission success. Accomplish the mission without undermining its purpose.

In dealing with captured enemies, the missions are to maintain control and to obtain valuable information. The fatal mistake, of course, is dehumanization—literally, murder.

Be Proactive and Responsive

The standard by which a leader is held culpable is whether he or she knew or should have known of a problem or of the potential for a problem.

So, when you become aware of a problem, fix it—fast. When you learn that people need help, help them—now.

Don't just wait for bad news to find you. The higher you rise in rank, the further you tend to be from ground truth. Inspect constantly and randomly, using yourself, your deputy, and your staff. Establish well-known, readily accessible channels for whistle-blowers; heed and protect them. Don't let your staff betray you by shielding the boss from bad news (as staffs are wont to do).

In all the cases of prisoner abuse, American leaders knew or should have known of the problems. Abu Ghraib, for instance, was a terrible assignment (e.g., Americans had to live in the prison, with far too few guards for the number of prisoners held, completely inadequate training, dismal quality-of-life considerations, and under frequent mortar attack), yet almost nothing was done to improve the situation.

Organization Is Important

Communicate what to do and what not to do clearly (orally and in writing if possible), through as many channels as feasible. Remember, studies have demonstrated that commander's intent often is misunderstood: check to see what leaders far down in the organization believe you expect of them.

Commanders tend to have too many transmitters and not enough receivers. Use your lawyer, chaplain, doctor/corpsman, and peers in other units to alert you to problems you might not have heard about through line subordinates. Seek information.

From the fact that prisoner abuse by U.S. forces happened in many places in a variety of units, we have reason to suspect that, generally, training was inadequate, expectations were unclear, and discipline was sometimes slack.

Resist Stovepipes

Fight hard for unity of command. No one should have any doubt who is in command—who lawfully can give them orders, and whom they must obey. Yet, despite the emphasis placed on this principle in war colleges, real-world experience regularly controverts this battle-proven counsel. In one unit's area of responsibility, other military units will conduct national tasking or special access program operations for which the first unit (including its commander) has no need to know. Various government agencies will be similarly active, along with many U.S. civilian workers (some armed) over whom the military has contractually specified, limited, or no authority.

Abu Ghraib offered all of these stovepipes: Brigadier General Janis Karpinski was in charge of the prison and directed the 320th Military Police Battalion, but she had no responsibility for nor authority over the interrogation center within the prison. Interrogations were conducted by the 205th Military Intelligence Brigade, by a plethora of U.S. government agencies (e.g., CIA, DIA, DEA, FBI), and contractor personnel (CACI, Titan). As Major General Antonio Taguba wrote in his report of Lieutenant General Ricardo Sanchez's command-relationship decision, this "effectively made an MI [military intelligence] officer, rather than an MP [military police] officer, responsible for the MP units conducting detainee operations."

Your people on temporary assignment elsewhere are still your people. Don't let them forget it: require that they be appropriately briefed before they depart your unit; direct that regular contact be maintained with them; and ensure that they have a secure, private channel to your command.

Be Professional

Military leadership, as Samuel Huntington, Morris Janowitz, Charles Moskos, and others established half a century ago, requires specialized knowledge of the command and control of violence, essential to the security of the society to which it is responsible, conducted by a recognizable and self-regulating group. Therefore, while you should respect the professionalism of the lawyer, doctor, nurse, chaplain, police officer, accountant, and many others who advise you or with whom you deal, your profession has its own duties and authority.

You must resist pressure to do what you judge to be unprofessional or unwise, no matter from whom it emanates; it's an essential element of your job description. Clearly illegal orders are rare, and obedience to civilian authorities is fundamental to the American military ethos. But gray comes in a host of shades, which only good judgment can discern.

Journalist Dana Priest mentions that, in late 1997, the administration wanted American pilots to be more aggressive in enforcing the southern no-fly zone of Iraq, including a requirement that they draw fire from Iraqi antiaircraft sites. Marine Corps General Anthony Zinni, leading Central Command, thought the idea militarily unsound. So when the Vice Chairman of the Joint Chiefs of Staff, Air Force General Joseph W. Ralston, told him, "They want you to do this," General Zinni replied, "Well, if someone wants me to do this, you can send me an order." No order was ever sent. As every military historian knows, General Zinni is not the only officer to have understood his professional obligations.

Your challenge of pressure to do what you deem clearly unprofessional or unwise might best be done face-to-face. Should your misgivings not be heeded, ask for written orders. And respond with written reservations about compliance. If your superior won't go on record in writing, think hard about whether it really is an order, and even harder about whether you must obey it.

Murphy Had a Point

Bad things happen: Plans aren't executed flawlessly, nature doesn't cooperate with your desires, people make mistakes, the enemy surprises you, and some critical component fails at the worst moment. Three things to keep in mind are: First, there are no permanent secrets ("[T]ruth will come to light," Shakespeare warned); second, trying to cover up a mistake is a worse mistake; and third (the Conspiracy Corollary), if something bad happens, many people will believe you planned that it happen.

Thus, what American troops did at Abu Ghraib was broadcast all over the world, the public reaction by U.S. authorities was slow and inept, and the nation's interests in the Muslim world (and beyond) were seriously harmed because many people think such behavior—having happened—must have been approved.

Culture Counts

Not everyone sees the world as we do. Fortunately, career military officers tend to be far more aware of this than their fellow citizens. Yet it remains a constant challenge to educate so many enlisted personnel, many on their first duty tours, to this fact's ramifications in daily operations. That challenge can and must be met by leaders, so what is achieved by fighting is not lost after victory.

Undoubtedly, Americans in uniform have interacted with many more Afghan and Iraqi civilians than enemy combatants. How we treat the former, and how they judge us, is as important as having defeated the latter in combat.

Watch What Your Bedfellows Are Doing

Nearby U.S. military units, other U.S. government agencies, civilian contractors, coalition armed forces, branches of the indigenous government, and representatives of international or other non-governmental organizations (including those providing humanitarian assistance) often have goals and purposes that differ from your mission. Their agenda and behavior may not advance, and perhaps to some degree thwart, your unit's objectives. Since you can't control these other actors on your stage, you must at least keep yourself abreast of their functions, goals, and intentions. Strive, of course, to coordinate your activities when collaboration can be fruitful, but bear in mind that some friends can be about as dangerous to you and your unit as any foe.

Any cursory review of the reports of abuse at Guantanamo or in Afghanistan and Iraq will suggest that bedfellows need careful scrutiny.

Don't Confuse Yourself

Neither your last promotion nor your present assignment made you the least bit smarter. You have more responsibilities, more difficult challenges, and the same 24 hours every day. You also have more subordinates to whom you can grant authority, from whom you can draw ideas and advice, and whom you can mentor. As the saying goes at Command Leadership School, "Command isn't about you." If you do it well, however, with your priorities rightly aligned, you'll realize the satisfaction of committing your whole self to your organization.

No matter where on earth you go, you remain a person responsible for your actions. War does not excuse you, and fighting terrorism does not absolve you. Resist the temptation to fight evil with evil, and do your utmost to support the integrity of all under your command. The warrior always faces two enemies: the armed foe he must defeat, and the evil within himself that he must control.

Images and impressions carry powerful messages. It sometimes matters more what people see and believe than what you actually do, so misunderstandings can overwhelm everything good you and your unit try to accomplish. A wise commander is attentive to details of what people see and think. Of course, while actually being moral cannot guarantee that you and your unit will be thought so, it's the only chance you've got.

Captain Grassey is the first James B. Stockdale Professor of Leadership and Ethics at the Naval War College in Newport, Rhode Island. He holds a BA in history from Villanova University and an MA and PhD in philosophy from the University of Chicago. He is a retired naval reserve intelligence officer and has been a life member of the U.S. Naval Institute since 1963.

13 "FIREPROOFING COMMANDING OFFICERS"

LT Lawrence Heyworth IV, USN

Detachment for Cause (DFC) of a commanding officer is always serious and has repercussions for the officer, the command, and the Navy. Two studies of DFCs conducted by the Naval Inspector General in 2004 and 2010 are summarized, noting that the reports found that "personal misconduct almost always outweighed other reasons for relief." Heyworth notes that if leaders fall prey to the myths of DFCs based on "bad apples" or "weak moral character," with a conclusion of "it can't happen to me," they misunderstand the complexities of leadership and ethics. He urges individuals and the institution to create a "systematic curriculum of character development" to foster character throughout a career in the profession of arms.

"FIREPROOFING COMMANDING OFFICERS"

By LT Lawrence Heyworth IV, USN, U.S. Naval Institute *Proceedings* (January 2014): 58–62.

A career built on solid ethics and character development is the best way to safeguard naval leaders from relief due to personal misconduct.

Naval officers relieved for cause have made headlines too often lately, with major newspapers highlighting the ethical violations and personal misconduct leading to such relief. Most recently, several post-command officers have been implicated in a Pacific Fleet bribery scandal.[1] Seeing these frequent headlines could cause many junior officers to develop a disproportionate understanding of the frequency of such events. Further, junior officers likely begin to question both the quality of our commanding officers and their own ability to avoid these same pitfalls, the details of which are rarely described at much length.

Statistics reveal no endemic problem with the Navy's commanding officers, yet these unfortunate incidents bring discredit to the service and more important, hamstring sailors by destroying command climate. Sailors deserve so much better from their commanding officers, and the law demands excellence as well.

Recent studies by the Naval Inspector General (NAVIG) and conclusions of contemporary psychologists indicate that while some systemic changes within the Navy may be beneficial, promoting the moral conduct of commanding officers should not begin as mandated training in a Navy school in the months before command, but should be ingrained through years of personal introspection and methodical shaping of one's character.

Crunching the Numbers

Secretary of the Navy Ray Mabus stated in 2011 that officers relieved for cause represent only a small percentage of the roughly 1,500 commanding officers in the service.[2] This would suggest that since 12 commanding officers had been relieved at the time he was interviewed, only 0.8 percent (12/1,500) were affected. Ultimately, in 2011 a total of 22 (1.5 percent) commanding officers were relieved for cause, including several for reasons unrelated to personal misconduct.[3] This would suggest that Navy-wide, commanding officers finish their tours with a 98.5 percent success rate. Does this tell the whole story? It may be helpful to examine one data set in greater depth to see if the success rate the secretary offers holds true when viewed in a different light.

If one were to consider only the commanding officers of the service's 285 ships, this narrows the total number of fired officers in 2011 to 9 (in 2012 this rose slightly to 11, while 2013 had seen only 6 at the time of publication).[4] Assuming an average command tour is 18 months long (as the majority are surface-ship commands), then throughout any given year there would actually be upward of 190 individuals in command. This estimate brings the percentage of fired commanding officers of ships for 2011 to 4.7 percent, or a 95.3 percent success rate.[5] Navy-wide historical data corroborate our focused approach: Small percentages are indeed the norm.

This seems to confirm the secretary's statement that only a small percentage of commanding officers are relieved for cause. It is worth noting that U.S. Code is incredibly demanding of commanding officers:

> All commanding officers and others in authority in the naval service are required to show in themselves a good example of virtue, honor, patriotism, and subordination; to be vigilant in inspecting the conduct of all persons who are placed under their command; to guard against and suppress all dissolute and immoral practices.[6]

Given this high, almost superhuman standard, could the current rate just be acceptable attrition? If the Navy were baseball, .953 would be a legendary batting average. A coach with a win percentage that high is unheard of. While a 2–3 percent failure rate could be viewed as insignificant or even praiseworthy in other arenas, screening boards highly scrutinize officers before selecting them for command at sea and all are expected to meet basic standards of personal conduct if they are to be trusted with billion-plus-dollar warships. Navy regulations state:

> The commanding officer . . . shall exercise leadership through personal example, moral responsibility and judicious attention to the welfare of persons under [his] control or supervision. Such leadership shall be exercised in order to achieve a positive, dominant influence on the performance of persons in the Department of the Navy.[7]

The failure to lead by personal example and the impact of a CO's relief can have far-reaching and long-lasting consequences for a crew of more than 250 sailors. A list of costs resulting from a commanding officer's relief for cause could include lost productivity from distracted or unmotivated crews, a loss of continuity of leadership, lower retention rates of disenchanted sailors, and significant negative effects on personnel management to redirect prospective commanding officers to the affected commands. Due to the cascading costs involved in even a single relief for cause, Navy leadership is correct in attempting to further reduce these events.

The Current Remedy

In 2004 and 2010 NAVIG conducted studies of detach-for-cause (DFC) events involving commanding officers. DFCs in 2003 were significantly greater than other years, and personal misconduct almost always outweighed other reasons for relief. However, no statistically significant trends or root causes were identified in the course of these investigations. The studies judged the personal misconduct to represent poor decisions on the part of the commanding officers and considered 2003 a statistical anomaly.

While neither the 2004 nor 2010 reports concluded a systemic problem exists, both focused on the disturbing rates of (presumably avoidable) personal misconduct reliefs and offered suggestions to improve selection processes and officer training. For example, the 2004 study recommended incorporating a 360-degree assessment tool at the prospective executive officer (PXO) level, developing and implementing a refresher course for all major command prospective commanding officers (PCO), improving operational risk management training in the surface warfare officer PCO pipeline, instituting command self-assessment training for all department heads and XOs, and reviewing for adequacy the training provided for PCOs.[8] Unfortunately, the 2010 study concluded that "the recommendations implemented as a result of the 2004 CO DFC study have had no discernible impact on the CO DFC rate, which has remained essentially constant since the completion of that study except for small year-to-year variations."[9]

Reliefs due to personal misconduct appear to be the avoidable DFCs, but the correct change to policy or tr events is not so apparent. The recommendations of tr reflect widely held assumptions as to why these commanders in personal misconduct: They are either simply "bad apples" or officers weak moral character who fall victim to an unfortunate but avoidable error chain. The logical solutions based on these assumptions would be an improved selection process to screen out bad apples and improved officer training to strengthen potential offenders' moral character. Contemporary psychology suggests that these assumptions are myths and that believing them can be detrimental to one's own propensity for ethical failings. Rather than attempting to modify existing Navy-wide selection processes and training, individual naval officers could personally avoid misconduct by a more complete understanding of why these situations occur.

Simply Bad Apples?

Dr. Philip Zimbardo of Stanford University adamantly refutes the bad apples myth by asserting that immoral behavior is observed when bad systems place good people in bad situations.[10] In his 2007 book *The Lucifer Effect*, Zimbardo evaluates an experiment he conducted in August 1971, the now-infamous "Stanford Prisoner Experiment" (SPE). In the SPE, a group of college-age men were randomly split into two groups: guards and prisoners. Although Zimbardo and his researchers were initially interested in what would occur psychologically to the prisoners, they soon found far more disturbing results in the guards. In the simulated prison environment where a guard's power was largely unchecked, prisoners were quickly and unquestioningly subjected to inhumane abuses.

Zimbardo concludes that abuses such as the ones witnessed in the SPE—and similar abuses chronicled at Abu Ghraib—are not the result of a few bad apples, but instead of putting *good apples into bad bushels*. In the context of the SPE, Zimbardo created bad bushels by placing guards without much training into seemingly consequence-free environments where leadership allowed inappropriate behavior to slowly escalate until it was out of control.

ne parallel to command at sea is not immediately obvious. In the SPE, ards existed to control prisoners and were often in direct conflict with them. As a ship's commanding officer, one is charged with the crew's training and well-being and is seen as the leader of a team. However, one striking similarity exists: A ship's captain, like the guards in the SPE, is often the ultimate authority in an environment isolated from many aspects of "normal" life. Navy regulations specify that "the responsibility of the commanding officer for his or her command is absolute . . . the authority of the commanding officer is commensurate with his or her responsibility."[11]

The bad-apple myth is especially easy to believe because most people assert these failings could never happen to them. Zimbardo addresses this directly, writing, "Instead of distancing ourselves from the individuals who were deceived by assuming negative dispositional attributes in them—stupidity, naiveté—we need to understand why and how people like us were so completely seduced."[12]

Naval officers (as PCOs) must pay special attention to Zimbardo's phrase "people like us." Ethical and moral training falls on deaf ears when students begin thinking, "This could never happen to me." To safeguard themselves from personal misconduct in command, officers must first convince themselves that moral failings can vex even the best individuals in a bad situation and must dismiss the myth of the bad apple.

Or of Weak Moral Character?

The second myth surrounding commanding officers' ethical failings is that those relieved for personal misconduct were not necessarily bad apples, but were probably of weak moral character. Contemporary business ethicists and philosophers suggest otherwise. In Dean C. Ludwig and Clinton O. Longenecker's *The Bathsheba Syndrome* we see instead that even the strongest moral character can fall prey to ethical failings when someone becomes successful.[13]

The Bathsheba Syndrome takes its name from the Biblical story of King David, a revered king who seemed to have it all—until he began an affair with a subordinate's wife, Bathsheba. David ultimately impregnated her and ordered his generals to ensure her husband would be killed in battle, which he was. The authors use this story to illustrate their theory that ethical failings in upper managers are not due to a lack of ethics training or a stressful, competitive environment, but rather are byproducts of success. In fact, they assert that personal and professional successes contribute to this vulnerability rather than demonstrate resiliency against it.

Ludwig and Longenecker suggest that four major factors contributed to David's personal misconduct, all of which can accompany success: privileged access, control of resources, an inflated belief in personal ability, and a loss of strategic focus. The correlations are obvious in this case: Every commanding officer has privileged access and control of resources by the nature of his position, and is therefore inherently likely to encounter the Bathsheba Syndrome. While the syndrome is taught at Command Leadership School to prospective commanding officers, junior officers, too, should be aware of these dangerous aspects of psychology so that they may strengthen their resistance against them.

It is important to note, however, that some contemporary psychologists think that even the strongest character may not be enough to avoid moral transgressions in many instances. David, for instance, was known to be a man of great courage (remember Goliath?). "Situationalists" would suggest—and are often supported by convincing data from experimental psychology—that the only way for David to prevent his affair with Bathsheba was to avoid private interaction with the woman entirely. Experimental results show that some situations seem to always result in immoral behavior, regardless of the character of the individual involved. Accordingly, officers must accept that their morality is never fully fail-safe and must learn to quickly recognize and steer clear of these situations.[14]

Building Character throughout a Career

The 2010 NAVIG study "uncovered no correlation between the likelihood of a CO to be relieved for cause and a CO's career path, personality traits as reflected in standard personality tests, accession source, time in command, or year group."[15]

This finding echoes the debunking of the two myths: There are no bad or weak apples. It then made several recommendations, the most significant of which was to create "an officer leadership training continuum from accession through major command."[16] This approach may yield positive results.

To prevent personal misconduct in command, officers must realize early in their careers that they will be highly susceptible to ethical failures when they are commanding officers. After shedding the "it could never happen to me" attitude, junior officers may then begin to strengthen their character through personal reflection.

Ideally, every naval officer would safeguard him or her self from ethical failure through deep and consistent introspection. Officers can begin to forge moral and ethical courage by reading classic philosophers' treatment of ethics (or even the works of more recent—and perhaps even more applicable—philosophers such as the late Vice Admiral James B. Stockdale) and then applying their principles to daily life. Insight can also be gained by reading about others' moral or otherwise courageous struggles; the Chief of Naval Operations' reading list is an excellent place to begin. Although reading provides perhaps the most solid foundation, inspiring movies and even conversations about motivating events can stimulate interest in moral and ethical courage. The key is then internalizing these concepts by asking, "How does this apply to me and my job?" This must begin as early as possible in one's career to lay the foundation for a lifetime of learning.

It would be folly to presume one could only read a few books and attend mandatory PowerPoint training offered by the Navy throughout a career of service and be safeguarded against ethical dilemmas that require the strongest character to identify and resolve. Any leadership continuum instituted in response to the 2010 NAVIG study must steer clear of rewarding "checks in the block" and instead focus on personal development. Philosopher William Durant once summarized Aristotle in saying, "We are what we repeatedly do. Excellence, then, is not an act but a habit."[17] Officers must consistently take the lessons learned and implement the theory behind them in their daily lives.

The 2010 NAVIG study advocated a centrally managed leadership curriculum, but this should not mirror existing courses of study. Character development cannot be taught, tested, or graded in a classroom. Existing schoolhouses should work to encourage personal reflection at early career milestones so officers have an opportunity to develop good ethical habits well in advance of command.

In surface-warfare-officer-school and department-head school, students (generally lieutenants) are divided into "wardrooms" of three or four and assigned an instructor "XO" (a post-department-head lieutenant commander) and instructor "CO" (a post-command commander or captain). These groups meet independently outside the classroom at scheduled intervals throughout the program to discuss important issues. Other schools should consider adopting this "wardroom" model—even for short periods of time—to encourage the personal development of officers. Even simple questions by a wardroom CO such as, "What book are you reading right now?" or "What accomplishment are you most proud of?" can nudge an officer toward deeper thinking. *The Lucifer Effect* and *The Bathsheba Syndrome* could both guide a lively dialogue. Situationalist experiments could be reviewed and parallels made to shipboard environments. These discussions are critically important at division-officer and department-head schools where students digest important concepts and then form good habits in their next tour at sea.

Officers complete nearly 20 years of professional development in most communities before assuming command, but most unrestricted-line communities do not even mention ethics in a classroom environment until prospective XO/CO courses. To rise to the moral and ethical challenges of command, an officer must impose upon himself a similarly systematic curriculum of character development. Only by admitting it could happen to each of us, recognizing situations where moral failure could occur, and subsequently developing strong ethical habits throughout a career can an officer safeguard against a relief in command due to personal misconduct.

Lieutenant Heyworth is a 2005 graduate of the U.S. Naval Academy, a 2006 graduate of Stanford University, and a surface warfare officer.

Notes

1. Thom Shanker, "Concern Grows Over Top Military Officers' Ethics," *The New York Times*, 12 November 2012; Craig Whitlock, "Navy's top ranks seeing turmoil," *Washington Post*, 18 June 2011; Craig Whitlock, "Two admirals face probe in Navy bribery scheme," *Washington Post*, 8 November 2013.

2. Whitlock, "Navy's top ranks seeing turmoil."

3. "Commanding officer, XO and senior enlisted firings," *Navytimes.com*, Gannett Government Media Corporation, 28 January 2013.

4. Ibid.

5. A ship generally has a new CO every 18 months, which means each ship has two COs every three years, or 285 ships. 2 COs/3 years = 190 COs per year; 9/190 = 4.7 percent.

6. 10 USC § 5947, "Requirement of exemplary conduct."

7. Navy Regulations Article 0802.

8. U.S. Navy Department, *Report on Commanding Officers Detached for Cause* (Washington, DC: Naval Inspector General, 2010), 1, 19–20. Hereafter NAVIG 2010.

9. Ibid., 3.

10. Philip Zimbardo, *The Lucifer Effect: Understanding How Good People Turn Evil* (New York: Random House, 2007), 445.

11. Navy Regulations Article 0802.

12. Zimbardo, *The Lucifer Effect*, 447.

13. Dean C. Ludwig and Clinton O. Longenecker, "The Bathsheba Syndrome: The ethical failure of successful leaders," *Journal of Business Ethics* 12, no. 4 (April 1993): 265–273.

14. Martin L. Cook, "Leaders of Character? The Dangers of 'Integrity,'" lecture, U.S. Military Academy, 29 October 2012.

15. NAVIG 2010, 3.

16. Ibid., 4.

17. William Durant, *The Story of Philosophy: The Lives and Opinions of the World's Greatest Philosophers* (New York: Pocket Books, 1991).

14 "CRITICAL DILEMMA: LOYALTY VERSUS HONESTY"

Joseph P. Hoar

Loyalty, honesty, and courage are ranked among the highest and most prized characteristics for naval leaders. Yet, as retired Marine Corps general Joseph P. Hoar astutely observes with respect to honesty and loyalty, "there is perpetual friction and competition between them." The higher one rises in rank, the more likely one is to face the dilemma of choosing between the two traits. Whenever the decision is faced, the leader must remember the oath taken to "support and defend the Constitution of the United States." Unwavering loyalty must be to the Constitution and not a particular person, unit, command, service, program, or department.

"CRITICAL DILEMMA: LOYALTY VERSUS HONESTY"

By Joseph P. Hoar, U.S. Naval Institute *Proceedings* (January 2005): 2.

The major conflict in the boardrooms of America is caused by the clash between loyalty and honesty. This was the issue I discussed with a friend as we shared pre-dinner drinks this past July—and his succinct appraisal of the state of American business resonated with me.

In fact, the tension between honesty and loyalty extends far beyond the business community and is raging in the U.S. government. An article in the *New York Times* of 3 October 2004 described how uncertainty and disbelief about the acquisition of an Iraqi nuclear capability were played in such a way that the Vice President, the secretary of State, and the National Security Advisor were able to assert publicly that an aggressive nuclear program was being pursued actively—when none apparently existed. Where were the Directors of the Central Intelligence Agency (CIA) and the Defense Intelligence Agency when the State Department intelligence office cautioned that the facts did not support this view?

Honesty has been a casualty in the past two years as the U.S. government made major errors planning and conducting the war in Iraq. Moreover, no one has been held accountable and there has been no acknowledgement of failure. President George W. Bush's characterization of the "catastrophic success"— aside from being an oxymoron—is a poor alibi for mismanagement of reconstruction.

During the past two years, while traveling in the Middle East and visiting in Washington, I listened to the steady drumbeats of retired and active-duty flag and general officers, foreign service officers, civil servants, and officials of friendly Middle Eastern governments: stories of spin and information suppressed, senior leaders enunciating desired goals and then tasking subordinates with finding facts to confirm those goals, promotion denied a CIA operative who did not come up with the "right answer" regarding Iraq's nuclear program, and offers of assistance in the search for peace and stability rebuffed because they came from "terrorist" or "axis of evil" states. Investigative journalists consistently uncover themes of bad news repressed by the government, which often uses security classification as the means of concealing embarrassing information.

No one is naive enough to believe this kind of behavior is new to Washington. But why should many military and civilian officials continue to favor loyalty over integrity? Arguments for loyalty in some cases are those of political affiliation and friendship. Further, disloyalty might well impede career advancement, retirement plans, home mortgages, and tuition for the kids. Finally, there is the argument that "I can do more to fight this kind of behavior inside the government than I can by resigning or going public."

The latter view was exemplified in 1971, when former Chief of Staff of the Army General Harold K. Johnson spoke to the student body of the Marine Corps Command and Staff College in an atmosphere of non-attribution. After some 40 minutes of describing the sad state of affairs related to the Vietnam War, an Army major rose to ask him why, given the unsavory situation in 1964–68, he did not resign. General Johnson responded to the effect that he could better deal with the problem inside the government than out. Years later, he regretted his failure to resign his post in protest.

In the U.S. military services, loyalty and honesty—often described as integrity—are highly prized virtues. They rank right behind courage as prized characteristics of an officer. Although there is perpetual friction and competition between them, we need go no farther than the oath taken by all military officers: "I solemnly swear that I will support and defend the Constitution of the United States against all enemies, foreign and domestic . . ." This provides the necessary direction as to where our primary loyalties should lie—to the Constitution, not to our commanders. As a matter of custom in the Marine Corps, officer promotion ceremonies include a renewal of that oath to underscore at each promotion that there are new opportunities to contribute. Equally important, it reminds officers their overriding fealty is to the nation.

Senior military commanders are most likely to face this dilemma. Because their responses are key to high-level policy decisions, they must realize that weighing honesty against loyalty is an abiding responsibility. When the history of the Iraq war is written, we can be sure that historians, journalists, and government officials will connect the dots dividing those who acted out of honesty and those who acted out of loyalty.

Retired Marine General Hoar, a former commander-in-chief of U.S. Central Command, heads J. P. Hoar and Associates, a consulting firm. He is a member of several boards, including that of the Center of Naval Analyses.

15 "CIVIL-MILITARY GAP: WHAT ARE THE ETHICS?"

Gregory D. Foster

Civil-military relations is a topic that is multifaceted and much discussed in classrooms, wardrooms, and professional conversations. It is an important subject but not one that is viewed with ethical concern. Yet, the author encourages readers to view civil-military relations through an ethical lens because democracy and the social contract upon which it is built creates an ethical imperative of civilian supremacy over the military. Foster argues that the social contract between the military, the leaders, and the people of a democracy, though unwritten, is an ethical compact and that failure to uphold its expectations endangers the compact and the nation.

"CIVIL-MILITARY GAP: WHAT ARE THE ETHICS?"

By Gregory D. Foster, U.S. Naval Institute *Proceedings* (April 2000): 82–86.

One of the most significant ethical issues facing the United States today is the current state of civil-military relations in this country. Why should the relationship between the military and society be viewed as a matter of ethical concern?

In the first place, the military's relations to civilian authorities and to society lies at the very heart of what democracy is all about. Harry Truman observed that "man has the moral and intellectual capacity, as well as the inalienable right, to govern himself with reason and justice." The eminent German sociologist Max Weber informed us that the state is defined by the government's monopoly of the *legitimate* possession and use of force. The military is the principal embodiment of state-centered and state-controlled violence. Thus, in a form of government where the people are supposed to rule, civilian supremacy over the military is essential—it is an ethical imperative. Where this relationship fails or falters, the very end of government stands in jeopardy.

Second, the three parties to the civil-military relationship—the military, its civilian masters, and the people themselves—are linked to one another by social contract. "The first principle of a civilized state," Walter Lippman observed, "is that power is legitimate only when it is under contract." A social contract is a tacit, mutually binding set of expectations, obligations, and rights. Because it depends on the ability—and the willingness—of the parties involved to live up to their end of the unwritten bargain, it is an ethical compact in every sense.

What Society Expects of the Military

The most obvious expectation of the military by society is operational competence—the ability of the military to fulfill its mission by accomplishing all assigned tasks. Should we judge or measure operational competence in terms of strategic effectiveness or mere military effectiveness? The importance of this question lies in the military's institutional preference—and its frequent insistence—that it be given only purely "military" tasks to perform, and that it be judged narrowly in terms of its ability to accomplish such presumably clear-cut tasks.

In another sense, the importance of this question lies in the realization that it is possible to be militarily effective without being strategically effective. In fact, experience demonstrates that military effectiveness, especially in the media age, can sometimes actually be strategically detrimental. A military, for example, that is structured, equipped, trained, and psychologically prepared to wage war for the purpose of securing peace—but whose presence feeds the insecurity and militarization of others—is strategically dysfunctional. Similarly, a military prepared only for the conduct of conventional war that can't be used at all when confronted by forms of conflict unlike traditional war is strategically useless. By extension, we might say that such a military, which is largely blind to a future waiting to be shaped, is an ethically debased instrument of state.

Is this what we must accept as the price of maintaining a permanent military establishment? Hardly. In attempting to measure up to expectations, the military should ask whether its true purpose is to prepare for and wage war, to prevent war, to provide for the common defense, to secure and preserve peace, or something else more ambiguously defined. These are fundamentally different aims, each calling for a qualitatively different force-in-arms to achieve them. Ours is a distinctly war-making military. Therefore, the military must question the deeply ingrained belief that the best, if not only, way to secure peace is to prepare for war. For too long we have uncritically accepted this classical shibboleth as received truth. The result has been the opposite of the permanent universal peace we want. To decline to even question such "truth" is itself ethically irresponsible.

Civilians also expect sound advice from the military—rendering the best possible professional judgment to the elected and appointed civilian authorities who are accountable for ensuring the country's security. Should this advice be *military* or *strategic*? Should the military be in the business of providing essentially unbounded strategic counsel on matters related to national aims and justifications, or should it restrict itself to more narrowly circumscribed military matters?

The answer has much to do with the fact that the politicians who enter office today are increasingly devoid not only of military experience and understanding but of strategic understanding as well. They frequently cannot answer even the "little" questions of what a military is for, much less the "bigger" questions of what a military *should* be for and to what effect. Such willful ignorance logically might be expected to lead to the disuse, misuse, or abuse of the military. Yet the Clinton administration and current Congress have shown that the result may well be the overindulgence of the military—evidenced by the continued profligacy of defense spending, as well as a cavalier overuse of the armed forces for nonstrategic, inappropriate, and even illegitimate reasons of political expediency and convenience.

Is it incumbent upon the military to fill this crucial intellectual void, especially if it profits from the ignorance of its overseers? Perhaps—provided the military is up to the task. Conventional wisdom has it that strategy and strategic thinking are an organic part of the military's intellectual domain. Is there some intellectual threshold, however, for those who have grown up professionally in a hierarchical institution governed by an ethos of obedience to authority, who have been forced to think technically and tactically, and who prize action over reflection?

A more commonly expressed fear is that permitting the military to be too centrally involved in determining national aims and policies is tantamount to politicizing the military, militarizing society, and creating the equivalent of a garrison state. Anyone even remotely aware of how thoroughly any propensity for the military overthrow of government has been socialized out of the U.S. officer corps will be quick to see that this is an unfounded fear. Were it otherwise, we might expect at least an occasional senior officer resignation over matters of principled disagreement with civilian authorities. And if we had a more strategically oriented military, the perceived threat would be even less worrisome.

Civilians also expect the military to be politically neutral—to remain above the unseemly expediency, favoritism, and self-interested dealmaking of low, partisan politics. Does that mean staying out of the high politics of statecraft as well? Not at all. Let us first recognize the impossibility of staying out of politics altogether. Even the public professions like the military and foreign service that most sanctimoniously trumpet their aversion to and distance from all things political thrive on the cut-throat bureaucratic politics of institutional natural selection. As Theodore White observed, "Politics in America is the binding secular religion." It defines who we are as a people; it energizes us; it is, more than we care to admit, our spiritual sustenance. More important, there is a qualitative difference of purpose between low and high politics. This distinction was probably best put by the career diplomat, Sir Humphrey Appleby, in the former BBC television series, *Yes, Prime Minister.* "Diplomacy," he said, "is about surviving until the next century; politics is about surviving until Friday."

From Washington through Eisenhower and Marshall, Americans have long revered the soldier-statesmen in our midst—uniformed professionals endowed not only with the expertise and virtues of their calling, but with the requisite political sophistication to appreciate the larger ramifications of their actions and to participate as an intellectual equal in the highest policy councils. Given the convergence that has occurred between the strategic and tactical realms of statecraft—where the seemingly most insignificant incident in the remotest corner of the globe can have almost instantaneous strategic reverberations at many spatial and temporal removes from its point of occurrence—the need for diplomats in khaki is every bit as great as that for diplomats in pinstripes.

No longer do we have "great wars" that provide a natural proving ground for the emergence of soldier-statesmen. Instead, we have desultory minor wars, whose frequency, persistence, and cumulative effects call for even greater men and women. What we now need, therefore, is to nurture a new breed of *statesmen-soldiers*—individuals schooled in the diplomatic arts, familiar with foreign cultures, practiced in the principles of statecraft, and able to integrate such know-how with a first-hand understanding of military culture, capabilities, and applications.

Finally, civilians expect the military to be socially responsible—to be an institution that not only gets the job done operationally, but that does so in a manner that contributes to civil society. Washington put things in proper perspective in saying, "When we assumed the soldier, we did not lay aside the citizen." In this country, none among us is a purely professional soldier. Those in uniform should be professional *citizen-soldiers* whose first allegiance must be to the society they represent and serve, not to the institution to which they belong. When the military becomes alienated from society; when its members talk of moral superiority but fail, in incident after incident, to walk the walk; when they evince a civil illiteracy no less pronounced and troubling than the military illiteracy they decry in their civilian political masters, the stage is set for a crisis in civil-military relations.

A Civil-Military Crisis?

Do we have such a crisis today? There are two schools of thought on the subject, now joined in lively debate. The most forceful arguments that there is a crisis have come from journalists Thomas Ricks, long of the *Wall Street Journal* and now with the *Washington Post*, and James Kitfield of *National Journal*. Ricks has contended that the military is becoming increasingly politicized and conservative, that there has been a disturbing decline in military professionalism, and that there is a widening gap between the military and society. He quotes retired Admiral Stanley Arthur, who commanded U.S. naval forces during the 1991 Persian Gulf War: "Today the armed forces are no longer representative of the people they serve. More and more, enlisted [men and women] as well as officers are beginning to feel that they are special, better than the society they serve. This is not healthy in an armed force serving a democracy."

Kitfield has echoed this position in referring to the "nearly unbridgeable cultural divide" between this nation's military and civilian leaders. He writes: "By nearly every measurement—recruitment, retention, equipment modernization, morale, readiness to fight—the all-volunteer force is in trouble . . . and those troubles can best be traced to the increasingly uneasy intersection of the military and mainstream American society." He quotes former Chairman of the Joint Chiefs of Staff (JCS) General John Shalikashvili, who has said: "I share deeply the concern that we are living through a period when the gap between the American people and their military is getting wider."

On the other side of the argument, the current JCS chairman, General Henry Shelton, recently stated: "There is a bond—a mutual respect—between our citizens and the military that few other nations can match. There has been a great deal written recently about the military becoming isolated from society. While I understand the concerns, I do not believe the people who wear the uniform of the United States are disconnected from the rest of American society or are in danger of becoming isolated."

Similarly, John Hillen, an appointee to the U.S. Commission on National Security/21st Century, takes the position that "the so-called gap between

American society and its military . . . has been misidentified and highly over-sold. No doubt, the values, beliefs, and patterns of behavior that define the cul-ture of military organizations are different from the culture of society in general. But I believe that most of America appreciates that difference, recognizing that the unique values and attributes of military culture are an occupational necessity for an institution tasked with winning under the unnatural stress of war."

There obviously are sound, defensible, well-reasoned arguments on both sides of this debate. We should not reject out of hand the proposition that there is a gap between the military and society. It could be that there is a crisis that demands our attention, but we just have not been perceptive enough to recog-nize it for what it is. There is no crisis in the conventional sense of a sudden occurrence of potentially catastrophic proportions that creates public alarm. It is more like a barely noticed lymphoma that feeds on itself and destroys silently from within.

With these characteristics, we should accept the alleged gap as something to be taken seriously, monitored, and managed. Hillen's comments in this regard offer room for discussion:

> This sort of gap needs to be managed, but it does not have to be closed. Eliminating the gap might solve the "problem" that the military does not look like society, but it might create a greater one—that the mili-tary will look too much like society. . . . If [the military] goes too far in pleasing the social mores of contemporary society, it may lose the culture needed for success in war. If it goes too rigidly in a purely mar-tial direction, it could create a praetorian force contemptuous of the society it protects with military disobedience toward civilian superiors being the first sign of trouble. (October 1998 *Proceedings*, pp. 2–5.)

This statement is problematic for three reasons. First, it suggests that there are clearly identifiable martial virtues that not only exist but are eternal in their content and relevance. Second, it alludes to a form of military disobedience that, if it occurred, would be flagrantly obvious, while ignoring the many subtle forms of disobedience that are so much a part of everyday bureaucratic politics. Third, the statement implicitly reflects a hypocritical hubris of many in uniform today, who consider themselves occupants of a moral high ground that overlooks an increasingly indolent, decadent, and even depraved society. For these self-anointed moral supremacists, the idea that there is a gap in values that is worth preserving has great appeal. This is a case worth making if the values to which the military subscribes are discipline, dedication, loyalty, propriety, and honor. But when those values become distorted—as they frequently do—into parochialism, resistance to change, insularity, workaholism, careerism, and aggressive intolerance and prejudice, then we have a military that not only is no better than society, but worse.

Needed: Strategic Leadership

Managing this gap, if in fact it exists, is a task for strategic leadership. Leadership is simply about exercising power over others—getting them to defer or go along with one's wishes. In contrast to coercive uses of power, leadership involves *inspiring* others to follow willingly. Such willingness derives from respect, which itself comes from setting an example of principled character and consistency. If we want to invest leadership with such purity of meaning, we could say that ethical leadership is redundant, while unethical leadership is a contradiction in terms. There are managers, administrators, executives, and commanders. But there are no unethical leaders.

Strategic leadership is distinctive in that it is a uniquely intellectual enterprise. "Reason and judgment," said the Roman historian Tacitus, "are the qualities of a leader." They certainly are the qualities of a strategic leader. Strategic leadership is not about position, nor is it about those intangibles that otherwise can invest one with authority, such as charisma, presence, or eloquence. It is very much about *vision*, that rare capacity that sets the strategic leader apart from his peers.

"Vision," said Jonathan Swift, "is the art of seeing things invisible." But vision involves more than just the ability to see what others can't. It is about more than just discernment or imagination. It is every bit as much about *courage* and *initiative*—a willingness to go out on a limb or to step outside the established norms, and to do so without prodding when it is not the accepted thing to do.

If the strategic leaders among us fail to manage whatever gap may have developed between the military and society, the greatest danger that lies ahead of the United States is that the military will become more estranged and progressively less responsive to the broader needs and aims of the country. The institution, complacent in the misplaced belief that the future necessarily must be a continuation of the past, will fulfill its own prophecy and flounder in self-induced entropy. Its members, themselves morally superior to the rest of society and technically superior to civilian decision makers who do not understand them, will equate the national interest with the self-interest of the institution. The flip side of this is that the military's civilian overseers, increasingly devoid of military experience and understanding, will defer unquestioningly to military judgment, thus turning the democratic ideal of civilian supremacy into a political reality of civilian subjugation and strategic incapacitation.

The greatest challenge before us as Americans will be to demand an institutional environment within our military that nurtures strategic thinking, responsible dissent, and the development of strategic leaders. For its part, the military needs nothing more to galvanize it in this regard than those most painful words about the military mind that H. G. Wells wrote in *Outline of History*: "The professional military mind is by necessity an inferior and unimaginative mind; no man of high intellectual quality would willingly imprison his gifts in such a calling." If there is truth to this indictment, the military's overriding aim should be to eradicate the condition. If it is false, the aim should be to set the record straight. Ethically and strategically, there is no alternative in the heightened ambiguity, turbulence, and danger of the post–Cold War world.

Mr. Foster is a professor at the Industrial College of the Armed Forces, National Defense University, Washington, D.C., where he previously served as George C. Marshall Professor.

16 "DEVELOPING THE WHOLE SAILOR"

VADM Thomas J. Kilcline, USN, with
CAPT Irv Elson, ChC, USN, and CDR Carlos Sardiello, USN

In a hard-hitting article on the responsibility of commanders to pro-actively engage in the full spectrum of professional development for those under their command, the authors link professional military ethics to readiness and mission accomplishment. They contend that there is a direct correlation between integrity and readiness and that to avoid the development of the former is to endanger the latter.

"DEVELOPING THE WHOLE SAILOR"

By VADM Thomas J. Kilcline, USN, with CAPT Irv Elson, ChC, USN, and CDR Carlos Sardiello, USN, U.S. Naval Institute *Proceedings* (July 2010): 52–59.

Recent integrity violations indicate a disintegration of values that could threaten Fleet readiness. Can commanding officers shape their Sailors' morality and character?

In the spring of 2008, two student aviators were taken to admiral's mast for several Uniform Code of Military Justice (UCMJ) violations stemming from an unauthorized flight in a Navy aircraft from Austin, Texas, to Naval Air Station,

Kingsville, Texas. What made this particular case stand out was the ease with which the students lied to cover the violation. This incident, along with several other disturbing professional-conduct violations that occurred near the same time, prompted me to reflect on the issue of integrity and its value to our Navy and compelled me to search for a solution.

Breaching the "Wall"

The Great Wall of China, built as an impenetrable defense against barbaric hordes to the north, is a magnificent structure. Many believed the wall guaranteed that no army could penetrate the country's borders. However, during the first hundred years of its existence, China was invaded three times. Not once was it torn down or scaled by invading armies. Rather, each time invaders entered by bribing a gatekeeper and simply marching through the gates. The Chinese had so relied on the physical integrity of the formidable stone walls that they overlooked the importance of ensuring the moral integrity of their soldiers.

In October 1992, then–Chief of Naval Operations Admiral Frank Kelso adopted honor, courage, and commitment as our Navy's core values. We still consider these traits essential to the task of integrating Sailors from different cultures and backgrounds in a cohesive and effective force. The process begins in boot camp and continues throughout a Sailor's Navy career. It is not a stretch to say, however, that teaching and affirming these values diminishes over time. One could argue that as our Sailors progress through the Fleet, the teaching of core values is replaced by our own "Great Wall" of rules and regulations. Boot camp drill instructors give way to Fleet supervisors, all of whom are focused on the challenges of their jobs. The intense interaction between drill instructor and Sailor gives way to busy commanders and a multitude of Navy instructions dictating proper behavior and procedures. Are these rules and regulations an adequate substitute for leaders who actively teach the value of integrity? Clearly, the answer is no.

Even a cursory reading of the news indicates that cracks have developed in our society's walls of integrity. A 2006 Gallup Poll showed that 80 percent of

Americans rated the moral condition of our country as fair or poor and thought it was worsening. These fissures are reflected in the Navy. We read in the press of senior naval officers being relieved of command because of moral failures. Even naval institutions struggle with the integrity deficit we observe in society. This year, for example, the Naval Academy witnessed the highest number of honor-code violations in 25 years.[1] This sobering statistic has prompted academy officials to review the honor code to determine how to better equip today's midshipmen to become principled leaders. While the moral condition of society and our Navy is subject to debate, one thing is clear: Our first and best line of defense should not be to rely on our "walls" of regulations, but on ourselves, as gatekeepers.

Where to Begin

An increased divergence from the Navy's core values degrades levels of readiness across the Fleet. Choosing wrong instead of right can result in catastrophic losses to personnel and equipment. For example, at the strategic level, the Walker-family spy case is a landmark breach of integrity and character that devastated the Navy.[2] At the operational level, when leadership is relieved for loss of confidence, it rocks a command to its foundation. Such situations force us to ask pragmatic questions. Are we, as Navy leaders, meeting our responsibility to teach integrity? Can and should we do so? And how do we tackle this task at every level of leadership?

In a 2008 essay entitled "The Whole Sailor" (see below), I attempted to answer some of these questions. Character underpins our humanity, and we should seek to nurture it in our Sailors. Ultimately, character defines a Sailor and has the greater impact on motivation and subsequent performance during peacetime or war.

"The Whole Sailor" was a lecture I first presented at the Naval Air Forces Senior Leadership (O-6) Symposium in March 2009. It was a first shot across the bow in tackling the role integrity plays in the Navy and in considering our responsibilities as leaders.

The question of where to begin is not an easy one. There is no consensus on the definitions of terms; even using the word "spiritual" in lieu of "moral" or "ethical" is controversial. Some leaders fear they will be perceived as endorsing one moral viewpoint over another. Interestingly, a recent CNO naval telegram (NAVGRAM) on family readiness used the term to describe Sailors' readiness: "Personal readiness [is ensuring] that every Sailor is physically, medically, psychologically, spiritually, and administratively ready to deploy worldwide."[3]

The Commanding Officer's Role

Six months later, the Whole Sailor concept was presented at our Naval Air Forces O-5 Commanders' Conference. The key questions the O-5s grappled with were how to "operationalize" the concept and how O-5 commanding officers can instill character and integrity in their Sailors.

With the help of Captain Rick Rubel, professor of ethics at the Naval Academy, an agenda was devised that included his lecture, "Why People Choose to Do the Wrong Thing." We reviewed the role morals play in making decisions and how integrity and character influence actions. In small group discussions, we followed the question of why good people choose to do the wrong thing with several others, such as how a CO can prevent people from choosing dishonorable actions and help Sailors develop their character and integrity so they will make good choices.

The results were surprising. While 80 percent of the COs believed they have a role in teaching integrity, 20 percent remained convinced that their role was one of simply enforcing the rules. They debated the chances of success in remediating Sailors who made missteps. A few felt that by the time Sailors reach the Fleet, it is too late or too difficult to teach integrity, particularly to a diverse Navy from many socio-economic, cultural, and ethnic backgrounds.

Despite the varied opinions, there was agreement on many things: by setting an example, demonstrating consistency among words, actions, and beliefs, COs generate trust. Many agreed that COs should set a high moral standard and identify ways to encourage Sailors to make honorable decisions according to self-chosen principles, even when leadership is not watching. They should reward good decisions, not solely reprimand errors and vices. And finally, they must be aware of the organizational pitfalls of bad decisions. The most important conclusion? Integrity doesn't just happen. COs need to demonstrate integrity—and to teach it at every level of their organization.

The Senior Commander's Role

The April 2010 Senior Leadership Symposium's format was similar, but focused on a commander's role in shaping the organization. We challenged our senior commanders to address assessment, guidance, and implementation. How can a commander assess the level of integrity of his or her command? What resources can be used to understand this aspect of command culture? How can we influence our organizations to create Whole Sailors? And what tools and processes are available to help our O-5s foster the process?

We determined that spouse participation would be integral to the discussion. Our effort was a natural extension of the recent CNO NAVGRAM mentioned previously, embracing the Navy family as an essential element to our Navy's success. We recognized that spouses play vital roles in the command's modeling of integrity. They were asked to consider how they could help promote the command's highest standards for its Sailors both at work and home. And finally, considering the role that the Sailor plays in shaping the "moral DNA" of the family, and vice versa, we asked, how do we move the organization from shaping the Whole Sailor to developing the "whole family"?

Our senior commanders felt that much was already established with respect to assessing commands in the area of integrity. Certainly, command-climate surveys have always been available. Both our O-5 and O-6 commanders thought Captain Rubel's presentation, "Virtues and Character—Strength Inventory," to be an invaluable tool, especially when combined with other resources, such as chaplains, who are experienced in taking the "integrity pulse" of the command. Whichever assessment tool is used, all agreed that face-to-face contact is critical. COs should capitalize on midterm counseling and fitness-report debriefs in the assessment process. Throughout the discussion it was clear that the Navy still has much to do to develop the right metrics to measure character.

Words and Deeds

During the symposium senior commanders recognized the need to routinely use the "language of integrity" in different command evolutions and to establish programs that recognize character and integrity, just as we recognize technical proficiency and expertise. Including these qualities as factors in Sailor of the Quarter/Sailor of the Year programs and recognizing Sailors "doing the right thing" during Quarters are just two examples. There is great value in talking about character in both positive and negative environments. Language is important, and words have meaning only if actions match those words. Across the board, Naval Air Forces' commanders agreed that leaders generate trust when their behavior, actions, and speech are congruent.

First Mates

Navy spouses considered their roles to be crucial in promoting principled actions by serving as examples of integrity and as family advocates. They recognized the need for educational programs on integrity and character as the key in developing "whole families." They also suggested that commands explore ways to maximize family integrity, because ultimately, the notions of the Whole Sailor and whole family are inseparable and should be pursued as an integrated concept.

In his keynote speech at the 2010 symposium, Dr. Michael Josephson, noted ethicist, author, and motivational speaker, introduced the Six Pillars of Character: trustworthiness, respect, responsibility, fairness, caring, and citizenship.[4] The results of Dr. Josephson's survey of the O-6 aviation commanders confirmed that our leadership believes that character and integrity do matter and can be taught. In the survey, more than 90 percent of the O-6 commanders agreed with the following statements:

- In taking an oath on enlistment, warrant, or commission in the U.S. Navy, Sailors assume the obligation for the highest professional and moral conduct in their professional and personal lives.
- Navy leadership should be more actively engaged in instilling, developing, and enhancing ethical and moral values to strengthen Sailors' characters and internal sense of right and wrong.

- Even though our Sailors come to us as adults, the Navy can influence their character, values, and ethics.

- The Navy should be involved in or concerned with what noncommissioned and officer personnel do on their own time or in their personal lives (including gambling, drug use, alcohol abuse, domestic violence, or marital infidelity).

Epitomizing Character

While the principles discussed here are not new and are perhaps self-evident, as a whole, naval aviation leaders who are exposed to the Whole Sailor concept understand it. It is my sense that by adopting it they will tread with greater confidence in the footprints of our forebears, such as the late Medal of Honor recipient, Vice Admiral James Stockdale. Admiral Stockdale epitomized the courage that is born of character. His years as a naval aviator set the bar for our moral and ethical standards.

Conversely, the Tailhook scandal of 1991 is recognized as a low point in American naval aviation. When one considers that virtually every one of our current squadron COs joined the Navy after that year, the importance of discussing the Whole Sailor with our commanders should be obvious. Numerous recent studies reinforce the principle that honest behavior can be fostered in an organization by reminding people of their values.[5] The dialogue is just as important as the concepts themselves.

In 1991, in the shadow of Tailhook, my father, Vice Admiral Thomas J. Kilcline Sr., who retired as Commander, Naval Air Force Atlantic, sent me a clipping of an editorial in the *Washington Times*. The author bemoaned the "moral illiteracy" in our country, writing that "[t]his should seem obvious to all of us, but it's not. And many young people today are equally at a loss to recognize the virtues of courage, temperance, honesty, generosity and charity."[6] She cited the book, *Virtue and Vice in Everyday Life: Introductory Readings in Ethics*, by Christina Hoff Sommers and Fred Sommers, which attributed this crisis to the deterioration of moral education and the fact that many parents never instilled in their children a moral center by teaching the difference between right and wrong. In the margin of the clipping, my father added this note: "I will never forget how disappointed I was that most COs were reluctant to discuss morals or ethics. [They] did not feel that they had the authority or that such things were their business."

Let's make it our business. With the military's increasing commitments and decreasing resources, the correlation between integrity and readiness is accentuated. We cannot afford the loss of readiness, materiel, or lives because of an integrity failure by one of our Sailors. The development of Whole Sailors and whole families is critical, and as commanders we must lead Sailors and empower Navy families to do the right thing.

Vice Admiral Kilcline relinquished command as Commander, Naval Air Force, U.S. Pacific Fleet, on 1 July 2010. During 37 years of service he led a Carrier Strike Group, Carrier Air Wing, and Fighter Squadron. He has more than 5,000 hours in Navy fighters.

Captain Elson has served as a Navy chaplain for nearly 25 years and is Force Chaplain for CNAP. He has done two tours at the U.S. Naval Academy and is a guest lecturer at the Naval War College.

Commander Sardiello is executive assistant to CNAP and Command Patrol Squadron Four Six (VP-46). He is a U.S. Naval Test Pilot School graduate with more than 2,800 flight hours.

Notes

1. *Navy Times*, 22 March 2010.
2. "The Navy's Biggest Betrayal," *Naval History* 24, no. 3 (June 2010).
3. CNO NAVGRAM Family Readiness 070233Z, February 2010.
4. Michael Josephson, *Making Ethical Decisions* (Los Angeles: Josephson Institute, March 2002).
5. Dan Ariely, "How Honest People Cheat," *Harvard Business Review,* January 29, 2008.
6. Suzanne Fields, *Washington Times,* 2 December 1991, Copley News Service.

Editor's Note

This article appeared within original *Proceedings* article:

"The Whole Sailor"

by Vice Admiral Thomas J. Kilcline, U.S. Navy

Crucial to the accomplishment of our mission is the comprehensive development of our Sailors, encompassing the fundamental physical, mental, and spiritual aspects of their humanity. We devote a great deal of time and energy in developing the knowledge of our Sailors, i.e., their mental capacity to accomplish their mission. Likewise, we promote and encourage their physical development and hold them to high standards in that arena as well. Recognizing that mental and physical development are but two-thirds of the equation, the question needs to be asked: What can and should we do as leaders to strengthen the development of the spiritual—defined in this context as the moral fiber of our Sailors?

The moral development of our Sailors depends on the development of their character, their internal sense of what is right and what is wrong. One only needs to look to Petty Officer Michael Monsoor, a Navy SEAL, who was posthumously awarded the Medal of Honor for saving the lives of two fellow Sailors. He is one of a select few Sailors and Marines who have earned our nation's highest military award. While these brave men and women came from different ethnic, cultural, and faith groups, the common thread that bound them together was character, that sense of doing the right thing. Character underpins the moral side of our humanity and we should all seek to nurture it in our Sailors. Ultimately, character defines who we are and has the greatest impact on motivation and subsequent performance in both peacetime and combat.

Character

The great force multiplier in our Navy is character; not technology, not numbers, but character. Character is the foundation of decision-making in the Navy. Character underlies courage in its most profound sense. While there may be some debate on the exact definition of character, there can be no doubt as to our moral principles. A man or woman of character is one whose existence rests on a solid moral foundation. This foundation sustains the Sailor during the greatest trials and crises and will provide the crucial moral orientation for decision-making at the moment of greatest need.

Seen in this light, the development of character becomes as crucial to mission accomplishment as is the development of our Sailors' mental and physical abilities.

Integrity

Integrity is an integral component of one's character. The Latin root of the word, *integritas,* originally referred to the soundness of the armor plate covering the breasts of the legionnaires of the Roman Empire. With integrity, all was possible in battle and all was whole. Absent integrity, there was vulnerability; indeed, there would be a "disintegrity" or disintegration.

Integrity is the unfailing trait that, above all others, a Sailor demands of leaders. They expect it of us. Absent integrity, there is no moral authority to lead. It is only when our Sailors see and identify integrity in those that lead them that we are able to demand and foster that same integrity from those who serve under us. As leaders at all levels, we must set the example with our goal of growing Sailors as people of integrity and of character. Our mission is dependent on Sailors making decisions based on foundations of solid values and beliefs.

Moral Conduct

In taking an oath upon enlistment, warrant, or commission in the United States Navy, we all have assumed the mantle of obligation for the highest professional and moral conduct. The American people have simply come to expect more from those of us in uniform. The father of our Navy, John Paul Jones, gave voice to this expectation in his expression of the qualifications of a naval officer. His words today echo sentiments that apply to all men and women in the Navy: "Every commander should keep constantly before him this great truth, that to be well obeyed, he must be perfectly esteemed."[1]

As leaders in the naval service, it is our duty and responsibility to help form Sailors and Marines who display such spiritual, ethical, and moral maturity that, even in the midst of the harshest of operational environments, they will continue to be people of honor who earn the pride of their families and our nation.

Just as we ensure our Sailors are mentally prepared and physically fit to accomplish our mission, we must also set the example and be the epitome of character and integrity. Our Navy's ethos of courage, honor, and commitment demands it, and we must in turn demand it of each other and of those Sailors we lead.

This essay includes excerpts of an unpublished paper, "Commandant's Intent," an address first delivered to midshipmen at the U.S. Naval Academy in 2002 by Lieutenant General John R. Allen, U.S. Marine Corps. It is excerpted here with permission of the author.

1. Written by Augustus C. Buell in 1900 to reflect his views of John Paul Jones (from *Reef Points: 2003–2004*, 98th ed., Annapolis, Md.: U.S. Naval Academy, 2003).

17 "LEADERSHIP FORUM: ZERO-DEFECT LEADERSHIP IS THE PROBLEM"

LCDR Erik Nyheim, USN

When discussing ethical failures of leaders it is easy to argue that the failure arose from "bad apples." It is also easier or more expedient to think that getting rid of "bad apples" will solve the problems. What is more difficult to understand and remedy is the potential of "bad barrels" that create an environment for "bad apples" to develop. Although he does not use the bad apples analogy, Lieutenant Nyheim argues that the prevalence of a zero-defect mentality in the Navy is detrimental to the development of naval leaders and to the institution. Not every poor decision need be a "career killer." The challenge for leaders and the military is to "foster a culture that values honesty and creates space to bridge failure and success" when appropriate.

"LEADERSHIP FORUM: ZERO-DEFECT LEADERSHIP IS THE PROBLEM"

By LCDR Erik Nyheim, USN, U.S. Naval Institute *Proceedings* (May 2016): 152–53.

The expansive effort to rid our service of failure has unintended consequences that detract from performance and character. Specifically, a fear of failure projected across the force robs leaders of the opportunity to teach service members how to learn from mistakes and grow. Rather than fostering a culture that values honesty and creates space to bridge failure and success, members often feel suffocated by the pressures of perfection. Those pressures, manifested in destructive ways, detract from our goal of being the finest Navy in the history of mankind.

John Wooden, legendary UCLA basketball coach, captured the essence of what can be feared from failure.

Let's face it, we're all imperfect and we're going to fall short on occasion. But we must learn from failure and that will enable us to avoid repeating our mistakes. Through adversity, we learn, grow stronger, and become better people.

Increased operational tempos, aging infrastructure, manpower and budgetary constraints, and contemporary challenges to global security already create enough stress on our service members. The addition of widespread zero-defect leadership—the pressure to be perfect—further degrades performance. We owe it to the nation and our people to do better.

I know this because those pressures and the coping mechanisms that followed could have cost me my career. Fortunately, I had strong leaders who showed me the error of my ways, valued self-awareness and growth, and helped me turn failure into long-term success.

Operational pressures from two wars combined with the pressure to be perfect led to poor decisions out of uniform. From binge drinking to questionable behavior, I could have lost the privilege to serve. Were it not for the focused attention of community leaders, expanded education on ethics and behavior, and congressionally directed mental and emotional health resources, I would not have recognized the destructive path on which I was traveling.

Feeling there was sufficient "safe space" to air failure gave me the impetus to reflect and improve. Through self-awareness and motivation, I was able to bridge failure and success. More important, however, the alternative culture that promoted honesty and improvement over perfection inspired deeper loyalty to my oath, our core values, and those serving around me.

This empowering leadership approach is worth spreading. It requires embracing an alternative view of failure. At my command, our leaders used deliberate communication that views failure as a learning opportunity. By opening a safe space for honest reflection on failure, self-awareness, and bridging to success [they] accelerated personal and professional development. Our command team delivered briefs that socialized our intent and solicited feedback from the wardroom and the chiefs' mess. These mid-level leaders, executors if you will, ultimately unlocked the potential of our service members. Their buy-in and trust were critical before we could inculcate this alternative leadership approach across the command.

Overcoming the zero-defect mentality required overcoming the inherent focus on perfection. To do this, we took the following steps:

- Change the perception and stigma associated with failure.
- Promote growth and improvement over perfection.
- Create the safe space that allowed personnel to bridge failure and success.
- Teach service members how to bridge failure and success by recognizing: Failure leads to reflection; reflection to self-awareness; self-awareness to adaptation; and adaptation to improved performance.

Two specific cases at my command stand out as examples of how the stress to be perfect resulted in failure.

The first case arose from a top-performing leading petty officer whose pressures to perfect his operational unit turned destructive. In his unbridled approach to succeed, his leadership style drove a wedge in the chain of command. He isolated himself from seniors, peers, and junior personnel. After a string of detachment liberty incidents exacerbated by alcohol came to light, leadership stepped in. Hard as it was, the leading petty officer had lost our confidence and was relieved.

As a top performer, he was wholly unaccustomed to failing. He did not recognize that the pressures of perfection had a counter-effect on the performance of the unit. Following a disciplinary review board, he was given a letter of instruction that started his bridging process. We told him if he chose to learn from his failure, he could turn it into long-term success.

The more he reflected on his actions, the more he became aware of how stress had manifested into failure. In time, and with deliberate leadership, he began to see the path to improvement. Months after feeling his career was over, he is in line to assume a leading petty officer billet in a new detachment. He is thriving again because our leaders allowed failure to be his stepping-stone to success.

The second case involved a young sailor whose actions out of uniform cost him his career. The pressures he felt to keep up as a new member in a special-operations environment led him down a path of substance abuse and poor behavior. When he was arrested for driving under the influence on a suspended license, those pressures reached a crescendo. After being informed that the service member had suicidal ideations, I immediately had him admitted for in-patient care.

When the sailor woke up in the hospital, I was at his bedside. I wanted him to know that despite his failure, there was a path to success, if he chose to take it. Despite the fact that his actions ultimately precluded him from continuing to serve, we still used the remaining time before his administrative separation to help him build the bridge to success. Through reflection, self-awareness, and a dedication to improvement, he bridged his path back. "It probably saved my life," he said to me before heading back into the civilian world, a better person for having learned from his failure.

These cases highlight the destructive way people are affected by stress that is exacerbated by zero-defect leadership. They also showcase how we can all choose to use failure as a growth opportunity. We can and must find ways to reduce the stresses of perfection and increase the safe space required for people to grow.

Lieutenant Commander Nyheim is currently an Executive Officer, and the Acting Commander of an East Coast–based Naval Special Warfare team. He was a 2015 Chief of Naval Operations Politico-Military Master's Program scholar and holds a master's degree in public administration from the Harvard Kennedy School of Government.

18 "ETHICS CAN BE TAUGHT"

A. Edward Major, COL Lee DeRemer, USAF (Ret.),
and LTCOL David G. Bolgiano, USAF (Ret.)

Few readers would deny that there is a connection between professional ethics and leadership. The deeper question is whether either leadership or ethics can be taught, and if so, when and how that should best be accomplished within the profession of arms. The present article focuses on ethics education at the service colleges and contends that personal ethics and professional ethics are overlapping domains and that teaching the latter at any level of service education or experience does not impinge upon privacy or the right to self-determination by the individual. The authors "advocate for continued and expanded ethics education by encouraging and equipping senior officers to better reflect on what virtuous and effective leadership looks like at the strategic level." Ethics can and should be a part of professional development throughout a leader's career and to ignore them is to risk personal and professional rocks and shoals for leaders at every level.

"ETHICS CAN BE TAUGHT"

By A. Edward Major, COL Lee DeRemer, USAF (Ret.), and
LTCOL David G. Bolgiano, USAF (Ret.), U.S. Naval Institute
Proceedings (December 2012): 58–62.

*Strategic leaders are made, not born—and a good place to train solid moral
and ethical officers is the Senior Service College system.*

In a May 2011 article in *Army Times*, Sergeant Ashley Moye, a 13-year Army
veteran, wrote, "We have tenets of leadership, leading by example, knowing your
soldiers, knowing your jobs, doing the right things and setting the example for
your soldiers. Today, those things are not done. Everybody gets the impression
that leadership is a trait we all possess. But it's taught, and we're not being
taught properly."

Moye is not the only soldier to recognize that servant leaders are much
better than self-serving leaders. General Martin E. Dempsey, the Chairman of
the Joint Chiefs of Staff, has also emphasized the need for developing senior
leaders with a strong ethical compass to better help them navigate the murky
waters of strategic leadership.

The challenges ahead of us in the 21st-century security environment man-
date that we reinvigorate our commitment to the development of strategic
leaders. We owe it to the nation to "build a bench" of leaders for tomorrow who
can operate at the highest levels of our government.

We need to be ready to add to the knowledge, skills, and attributes of our
brilliant tactical leaders and prepare them to operate at the strategic level. Pos-
sessed of a strong personal and professional ethic, strategic leaders must be able
to navigate successfully in ethical "gray zones," where absolutes may be elusive.[1]

General Dempsey connects the gray zones of personal ethics to professional
competence in his call to action. But how are ethics taught for such an amor-
phous subject? Some contend that this topic is a personal matter and that, in
teaching it, we are intruding on soldiers' privacy and right to self-determination.
Ironically, some of these people are ethics professors. We disagree and believe it

is possible to meet the general's challenge—at any level of professional education. An ethics education is well worth the time and money, for the reasons we offer here.

A Higher Standard

Putting these concerns in simple terms, the honor code at the U.S. Military Academy states, "A cadet will not lie, cheat, steal, or tolerate those who do." This may be enough for an officer to successfully navigate at command levels all the way to brigade command, but more study and reflection are needed at the succeeding levels of one's career.

Major General Gregg F. Martin, president of National Defense University and former commandant of the U.S. Army War College, seconds Dempsey's admonition. In his opening note to the informational booklet "U.S. Army War College: Developing, Inspiring, Serving Strategic Leaders," he states that "refining ethical decision-making" is essential to the holistic development of senior military officers that is the objective of the Army War College. The strategic leader cultivates 'values-based, ethical climates' to be "ready to make decisions in a volatile, uncertain, complex, and ambiguous, environment."[2]

Some may argue that if, after 20 years of service, an officer does not have his basic moral compass in order, then no amount of education or training can correct it. Even if true, this assertion misses the point. First, the services should identify and remove people who have made it through two decades with a flawed understanding of the role of ethics in the life of a professional. The failure of a few should not prevent good leaders from being educated with the expectation that they can become even better. We advocate for continued and expanded ethics education by encouraging and equipping senior officers to better reflect on what virtuous and effective leadership looks like at the strategic level.

Instilling Virtues

Leadership instruction necessarily involves the teaching of virtues. Alexandre Havard, in his book, *Virtuous Leadership: An Agenda for Personal Excellence*, argues that virtues "are part and parcel of [professional competence] and substantially so." Professional competence implies the application of technical knowledge to some "fruitful purpose."[3] The officer-students in the Senior Service College (SSC) system have already proved their technical competence. They attend SSCs specifically to study strategy and leadership to raise their competence to new levels.

The United States requires virtuous senior officers whose decisions reflect well on their profession and inspire trust and confidence in their countrymen. Preparation and background for the challenges of general officership entails education. As Havard writes, "Virtues are qualities of the mind . . . that are acquired through repetition. Leaders either strive to grow in virtue . . . or they are not leaders."[4] Because SSC students are transitioning from tactical to operational and strategic leadership and staff positions, the SSCs are the most obvious and propitious avenues for such education.

Recently some authors have criticized the structure and even the necessity of the military's SSC system. They charge that the SSC curriculum is neither academically rigorous nor effective in teaching students how to think versus what to think. Air War College professor Daniel J. Hughes writes: "By and large, there are no real academic standards, a fact to which new professors quietly object but which they, like the older hands, eventually accept with resignation tempered with dark humor. To use an old cliché, students and colonels have a tendency to stress what they need to know in an immediately practical sense, while the professors are more interested in how to think about issues of policy, strategy and so forth."[5]

Professor Richard H. Kohn of the University of North Carolina Chapel Hill, is similarly direct: "Related to these strategic and political failures are possible moral deficiencies among the officer corps, which have arisen in the last few years. At its heart is a growing careerism that has led to micromanagement from above and a sense that any defect will derail a career, which in turn leads to risk aversion and sometimes to cover-ups, avoidance of responsibility, and other behaviors that harm the ability of the armed forces to succeed in battle."[6]

Kohn, however, ranks moral deficiencies third behind a lack of intellectual rigor and political savvy. While his arguments are sound, the lack of moral structure and virtuous leadership may be the preeminent factor driving the other two problems. Moreover, the recent ethical scandals at the senior-most levels of military leadership belie Kohn's ranking of these issues.

Strengthen the Curriculum

While some critiques of the SSC curricula often reflect a misunderstanding of the diverse schools' roles and missions (as well as of military culture), they nevertheless deserve our attention. We suggest a reconsideration of two items: ethical reasoning and critical thinking. The U.S. Army War College's core curriculum contains only six hours dedicated to teaching ethical reasoning and philosophy. Additional time in the curriculum is allotted to applying these foundational lessons in the context of senior leader responsibilities, but this is not sufficient.

One shortcoming in leadership development is in the field of ethics, a deficiency often caused by the convenient substitution of legal briefings by Judge Advocate General (JAG) officers both at the installation and staff levels. The law is never a substitute for ethics, and we do a great disservice when our education methodology implies or demonstrates that we fail to understand this nuance. Moreover, an act is not ethical just because it's legal. As Plato stated in *The Republic* when he described the ideal leader or philosopher-king: "I need no longer hesitate to say that we must make our guardians philosophers. The necessary combination of qualities is extremely rare. Our test must be thorough, for the soul must be trained up by the pursuit of all kinds of knowledge to the capacity for the pursuit of the highest—*higher than justice and wisdom*—the idea of the good." (Emphasis added.)

The legal system is often a regressive review of events that have already occurred. It is meant to demarcate unacceptable behavior and punish those who do not conform to its standards. The law is rarely an inspiration or command philosophy, such as SSCs aspire to offer in training our country's future general officers. Sadly, too many senior leaders now boast that they never make a decision without first consulting their judge advocate. The purpose of the SSC education is to look forward and prepare for future challenges and conflict resolution. Therefore, the teaching of ethics must be seen as a means to reinforce our nation and our profession through reflection, application, and case studies of values that we treasure as Americans.

In their article, "The Army's Professional Military Ethic in an Era of Persistent Conflict," Don M. Snider, Paul Oh, and Kevin Toner argue that there are two types of moral foundations in the Army ethic: institutional and individual.[7] They contend that moral teaching is a vital part of establishing an ethic for soldiers and the moral/individual foundation is essential to the effectiveness of the Army (and broadly for the military) as directed under Army Field Manual 1. These foundations are requisite, but individual moral training is essential for those in strategic decision-making roles.

Some claim that the SSCs may teach institutional ethical values, but not individual ethics, which would represent a constitutional invasion of privacy and a personal intrusion. Neither the law nor common sense supports such an argument. Taken to its logical end, this argument would have to deny the instruction of both individual and institutional ethical values, since the institutions that frame our conduct through culture, climate, and policy necessarily will have an intrusive effect on individuals. Teaching anything else becomes moral relativism. Better to call nonsense what it is and move forward responsibly.

SSCs can cultivate intuition and understanding through ethical education, which is the best way to teach a moral set of values. It might fall out of vogue, but it never loses relevance. Using the Army as an example, "its evolving expert knowledge in the moral-ethical domain is what allows the profession to develop individual professionals—soldiers and their leaders—to fight battles and campaigns 'effectively and rightly,' as expected by the client the profession serves."

Navigating the Gray Areas

The challenges of our times also suggest the need for ethical education. Persistent, low-level conflicts that often more resemble police actions than combat, such as our current engagements in Iraq and Afghanistan, place tremendous demands on individual soldiers and their understanding of ethics.

Theories of moral development help explain how individuals process such conflicts and their capacities for doing so. Much of this analysis focuses on moral quandaries between personal values, such as "fight-or-flight" reactions that arise during stressful situations, which might include combat or high-stress command or staff billets. (It is not unheard-of, for example, for a senior leader to ignore an impossibly complex decision rather than grapple with it: consider the lack of Phase IV planning for the invasion of Iraq.)

A theme that arises in these studies is that the capacity to make ethical decisions requires moral courage and the efficacy to carry them out. Much of this is won by identifying with the institutional values of the armed services and the institutional reinforcement of these values by aligning its [the armed service's] actions with its statements. But the teaching cannot end there. To act on these values, the individual must develop the sufficient will to convey that value into action.

Ethical education assists with the maturation and moral engagement of a senior officer's understanding of dilemmas and complexity of understanding, which he and those under his charge will encounter when serving in the field.

The moral resolutions we wish to encourage are made only where the service members possess an innate sense of ethics. Ethical education at the SSCs can be designed to prepare senior officers to act in a manner consistent with our shared American values and the responsibilities of their office. Following Major General Martin's precept that ethical education is essential for development of senior officers, the SSCs should seize the opportunity to improve the depth and breadth of the ethics education their students receive.

As leaders rise in responsibility, expand their scope of power, and engage a faster and increasingly complex world, the challenge gets harder. SSC curriculum can do a better job of preparing our officers for that world. Here are some options:

- Add more philosophy to the SSCs' core curriculum. There is a reason Plato, Aristotle, Thomas Aquinas, John Locke, Thomas Hobbes, and others are the foundations of what we once called the classics of Western civilization: They have stood the test of time. They're still relevant. Add to Western philosophy the works of Eastern and south

Asian philosophers, and we can build a study of the history of ideas that can enrich American and international SSC students' experience with a global and cross-cultural exploration of the enduring themes of civilization.

- Inventory our case studies to the core SSC curricula with the express purpose of exploring ethical dilemmas that senior military leaders faced. Develop case studies to facilitate seminar discussions on key topics for which our courses have gaps. History is replete with scenarios we can apply to any of the core courses in any of the nations' SSCs.
- Add an elective on philosophy. Most members of the military profession will be pleasantly surprised to see how much interest they now have in a course that so many disliked when they were a generation younger.
- Develop a Great Books curriculum alternative that provides select students the opportunity to revisit the literature that has informed and challenged leaders and thinkers for centuries. Offer it during a significant portion of the academic year with an exception from some of the otherwise required curriculum objectives.
- Offer a recurring series of brown-bag lunches to interested students and faculty with the purpose of building a foundation of the philosophy of ethics and building on that philosophy with a series of case studies for dialogue. This has already been especially effective in some SSCs.

Our nation invests heavily in its military leaders, often with admirable results. Having been trusted so deeply, we should constantly refine our curricula to prepare these senior leaders to the best of our ability. The opportunity of ten months in-resident education is the envy of every public and private organization. The challenge to the SSC officer will include, more than anything else, the ability to apply judgment and perspective to a wide array of national security tasks. Unfortunately, the SSCs are currently spending more time on learning the tasks and less time on developing judgment, perspective, and the ethical development of senior leaders.

Colonel DeRemer taught ethics and strategic leadership for five years at the U.S. Army War College. He is now a leadership and strategy consultant with Booz Allen Hamilton and a doctoral candidate at Benedictine University.

Mr. Major is an attorney in private practice admitted in New York, New Jersey, and Florida, as well as in the United Kingdom. He has published several articles in the *Military Review* and with the Strategic Studies Institute and the Center for the Army Profession and Ethic.

Lieutenant Colonel Bolgiano is a former paratrooper, police officer, and faculty member at the U.S. Army War College. He is the co-author of *Fighting Today's Wars: How America's Leaders Have Failed Our Warriors* (Stackpole, 2012).

Notes

1. GEN Martin E. Dempsey, "Building Critical Thinkers," *Armed Forces Journal*, February 2011.

2. MG Gregg F. Martin, "U.S. Army War College: Developing, Inspiring, Serving Strategic Leaders," U.S. Army War College publication, 2011, 2.

3. Alexandre Havard, *Virtuous Leadership: An Agenda for Personal Excellence* (New York: Scepter Publishers, 2007), xvii.

4. Ibid., xvi, xiv.

5. Daniel J. Hughes, "Professors in the Colonels' World," chapter 10 in *Military Culture and Education*, ed. Douglas Higbee (Burlington, Vt.: Ashgate Publishing, 2010).

6. Richard H. Kohn, "Tarnished Brass: Is the U.S. Military Profession in Decline?" *Army History*, Winter 2011, 27.

7. Don M. Snider, Paul Oh, and Kevin Toner, "The Army's Professional Military Ethic in an Era of Persistent Conflict," Strategic Studies Institute, Professional Military Ethics Monograph Series, October 2009, 11.

19 "THE FLAWS OF LEADERSHIP BY EXAMPLE"

LT Dustin League, USN

Naval history is full of heroic models of leadership who epitomized integrity, honor, courage, and commitment. Their lives and service should be well known and recounted often. In this essay Lieutenant League encourages readers to do just that, but he warns that focus solely on these leaders for an understanding of leadership is insufficient for the military professional. Even great leaders and heroic models have flaws. Therefore, the prudent naval leader will not just mimic the heroes, he or she will dive deeper into their history to learn the principles upon which their actions were constructed and then use those principles to create a personal and professional leader identity.

"THE FLAWS OF LEADERSHIP BY EXAMPLE"

By LT Dustin League, USN, 2013 Leadership Essay Contest
Honorable Mention, U.S. Naval Institute *Proceedings*,
www.usni.org/flaws-leadership-example.

Leadership is the lifeblood of the U.S. Navy. There is nothing that can be attributed to a person that is more highly valued, lauded, or sought after in our organization. From the first day of boot camp to every change of command and

139

retirement ceremony, leadership is preached as the ultimate personal quality. For a term we use so freely, we also spend an inordinate amount of time debating its nature. Because it is the core tenet of our organization, one might expect that we had solved the puzzle by now. Instead, we argue over whether it can be taught or is innate, how it can be intrusive or empowering, and what other traits contribute to it. What is it about leadership that makes it so much harder to define than the attributes so often associated with it, such as charisma, efficiency, intelligence, ambition, and morality?

I believe we struggle to find a common definition because we all relate to leadership in different ways. We all choose our heroes and grapple with the question of leadership through their example. Those heroes may be personal—family members or those with whom we have served—or historical, even drawn from fiction. It is only natural that we gravitate toward heroic models that resonate for different reasons, but because of this we have failed to find a concise definition.

My father is a carpenter and architect, and my education was in physics and engineering. By temperament and training, I prefer to deal with root causes and fundamental principles, building up from them instead of applying individual cases across a broad spectrum. While it is possible to find success in leadership by emulating predecessors, imitation does not substitute for genuine understanding. To truly grasp leadership, I have embarked on a journey to find its root principles. History and literature gave me models to follow and heroes toward whom to aspire, but it was in philosophy—the philosophy of the *Meditations*—that I found the fundamental nature of leadership: selflessness.

Imperfect Heroes

Historical heroes fail to illuminate ideal leadership because they are never perfect. For every great leader used as an example, there are flaws. We build up the "great men" and women by cherry-picking their success and positive attributes, while pushing their failings into the corners. Lord Horatio Nelson is lauded for his inspiring command at sea and his victories over the French, but his affair with Lady Hamilton—surely a failure of loyalty and honesty—are glossed over. Some argue that his personal failings are immaterial to any discussion of his leadership ability. But if that is the case, why did General David Petraeus suffer such a backlash when his extramarital affair was discovered? Similarly, if we were to hold up General Stanley A. McChrystal for his battlefield leadership, any discussion would have to separate his positive attributes from his lapses in judgment portrayed in the *Rolling Stone* article that ended his military career.

No individual throughout history can stand up to intensive scrutiny without having some flaw or failing revealed. So there is no perfect, single example on which to base our idea of leadership. We are forced either to ignore unpalatable traits in our heroes or study them piecemeal, putting the laudable to one side and the disgraceful to the other. George Washington and Thomas Jefferson both kept slaves; John Paul Jones was fired from Russian service over accusations of rape and admitted to employing a prostitute; Admiral Hyman G. Rickover was abusive to subordinates and insubordinate to the civilian authorities over him. Even legendary and mythical figures fail to live up to the ideal: the stories of King David gave us the Bathsheba Syndrome, and King Arthur was slain by the offspring of his own incest. This is not to say that these were not good leaders, but instead to show that none of them embody the perfect ideal of leadership. For me, trying to become the best leader I could by looking to historical models felt like trying to build a cathedral by looking at pictures of St. Peter's Basilica and copying it: even though I could make a façade that was similar, I could never hope for it to survive if I didn't understand the architectural principles involved.

Fictional Examples

Of course, the study of historical leadership models is not without merit. They serve a necessary purpose in translating the ideal into a more concrete and teachable mode, but it is important to understand their limitations. History should also not be our only source for material, because it comes fraught with all the petty failings of real individuals. Better, in some ways, are examples drawn from literature and the arts, because there individuals can be formed without defects or flaws; they are the architect's concept drawing rather than the blueprint or the building.

Modern cinema offers two examples of what I see as the ideal leader, both from writer-director Ridley Scott. His epics *Gladiator* and *Kingdom of Heaven* present heroic leaders who demonstrate moral judgment and selfless devotion to causes, putting aside their own lives, honor, and glory. In *Gladiator*, Maximus Decimus Meridius is shown to be a powerful and respected general—his authority and potential influence are feared by Commodus—but in his discussions with the Stoic emperor Marcus Aurelius (a name that will come up again), he demonstrates that he cares nothing for the trappings of power, has no need to assuage his ego, and serves only for the "dream of Rome." His desire to escape execution is not for any thought of his own life's worth, but for his family, and when he is finally victorious, his only command to the Praetorians is an attempt to restore that dream of Rome.

Kingdom of Heaven presents an even clearer example in the "perfect knight" Balian of Ibelin. Balian constantly makes the honorable decision regardless of the personal risk or cost to himself. He spares the life of his enemy, refuses to plot against his allies, and defends Jerusalem to protect its people. Balian defies every cynical suggestion that he take power for himself, including turning down King Richard the Lionheart and denying his own valor to strive toward his "Kingdom of conscience, or nothing." When he has done everything in his power, achieving an unexpected moral victory, he willingly fades from public view without hope or desire of accolades.

Both these examples demonstrate heroic leaders capable of devoting themselves wholly to their cause and putting all their ability into its service, not for any hope of advancement or personal reward but because the cause itself is just. In many ways, literature and the arts bring us closer to the ideal leader and dramatize examples in a way that resonates with us. But we are still just looking at a finished product and trying to copy it instead of understanding it.

Reexamining the Criteria

Top-down definitions failed to give me the understanding of leadership I needed, so I attempted to focus less on the heroes themselves and drill down on what are considered their merits, to pick traits considered worthy and use them to construct a foundation. This too seemed lacking. It failed me because you cannot build something without knowing what it should look like at the end. It failed because to pick traits and use them to define leadership was to mistake the tools for the carpenter. Leaders are not defined by their charisma, ambition, or effectiveness—or they should not be—leaders are defined, or recognized, by their successes, which is everything they use to accomplish it. This is not to say ends justify means. But we must recognize that we are in an organization that requires mission accomplishment. Any model of leadership that fails to account for this is terminally flawed. What must be understood is that no single tool can be used to define great leadership. Each attribute taken alone or in the wrong proportion will lead to a flawed leader. Just as we can find defects in all historical heroes, we can find imperfect leaders who exemplify all of our prized traits.

If it is success for which our leaders must be shaped, then surely effectiveness should be the principal trait by which they are judged. Yet history is replete with examples of leaders who were highly effective but also deeply, if not horribly flawed. General William Tecumseh Sherman was perhaps the most effective of the Union generals during the Civil War; his drive across the Confederate states crippled their warfighting capability. But the same savagery that brought him such success has also made him a controversial figure, to say the least, and one rarely praised for his leadership. An even more drastic example is Vlad Tepes, who was very effective at keeping his Ottoman enemies out of Wallachia but has gone down in history with an unmatched reputation for cruelty.

Clearly we do not value success at any cost. We want leaders who win in ways we consider honorable. Ambition or drive is often considered an important trait, but the ambitious and flawed leader is even easier to unearth than the effective and flawed. Alexander the Great was both, but his ambition was perhaps his single most defining trait. There is scant evidence that he was motivated by anything other than personal drive, especially for his later campaigns in India and those planned for Arabia. Alexander was a man who willingly accepted, even encouraged claims of his own divinity; he killed one of his own lieutenants after that man disparaged his achievements. He led thousands of men across the world for no greater purpose than conquest. Alexander the

Great is still praised for his leadership skills and achievements, but never universally; he is the epitome of the flawed "great man" of history.

The ability to inspire, to rally support behind oneself, is seemingly the very definition of leadership. But this is not the description that the U.S. Navy needs for *good* leadership. It is merely one tool that an ideal leader must have. Both Martin Luther King Jr. and Adolf Hitler had it, but only one of them should be even remotely considered a good leader. These are just a few examples of how seemingly laudable traits do not necessarily result in great leaders, and why building a framework for the ideal on such a basis is a faulty premise.

Back to Philosophy

Learning from historical and fictional examples helped provide an idea of what a great leader looks like, but the lens were always distorted. There were obviously some root principles at work, but the hero's flaws obscured them. My education in physics and the Navy's nuclear-power training pipeline had instilled in me a deep desire to understand everything down to its most basic principles. It is possible to create a perfect copy of something that will function; a recreation of St. Peter's Basilica will stand. But you will never be able to build something new unless you understand why the original worked. I had to find a way to grasp the fundamental principles of a human concept. This is when I turned to philosophy and, perhaps not coincidentally, found my answers coming from another character in *Gladiator.*

Marcus Aurelius was, according to Machiavelli, the last of the good emperors, known as a philosopher-king even within his own time. Today he is still regarded as one of the greatest Stoic philosophers. His achievements as emperor are noteworthy, but to take his accomplishments and life as my role model would be to fall into the same trap against which I argued earlier. It was not Marcus' life that I found so illuminating, as much as his writings. In his *Meditations*, he describes the ideals by which he strives to live. This is the method of understanding leadership that most appealed to me, this exploration of guiding principles. Philosophy, particularly Stoic philosophy, gave me the understanding that I needed to construct a concept of ideal leadership.

This is not to say I have lived up to it, but through its study, at least I now know toward what I am striving. I understand why St. Peter's Basilica stands, and I can use those principles to build my own cathedral. I can build a leadership style that reflects my personality, traits, and abilities, knowing that it is fundamentally strong. The principle that I found in Stoic philosophy, and that I believe is the core of good leadership, is selfless service.

The Ideal Leader Is Selfless

Duty was everything according to Marcus Aurelius:

> Let it make no difference to thee whether thou art cold or warm, if thou art doing thy duty; and whether thou art drowsy or satisfied with sleep; and whether ill-spoken of or praised; and whether dying or doing something else. (*The Meditations of Marcus Aurelius,* trans. George Long, vol. 2, part 3, Harvard Classics, 1909–14.)

In Marcus' philosophy, a leader should never be concerned with rewards or the praise that might come from success. He should concern himself only with doing what is best for the state he serves. This is selflessness. It is the abandonment of ego and pride to the cause that is greater than oneself. In the Navy we are called upon to serve the will of our nation, not ourselves, no matter what is our position. The more we set aside our own pride and ambition in service of that duty, the better we are able to achieve ideal leadership.

Alexander the Great was filled with his own ambition and pride, but an ideal leader has only one ambition: to serve his state. The success of the mission is not important as a way to prop oneself up or satisfy one's own vanity. It is important because that is all the ideal leader exists to do. The leader must see that his only importance is as a facilitator for the successful completion of his tasks. The U.S. Navy is itself merely one tool in the hands of the government of the United States of America. How much more must the leaders within that organization see themselves merely as instruments of the U.S. Navy.

The ideal leader is willing to sacrifice everything of himself to his mission and to ask nothing in return. Napoleon Bonaparte's invasion of Russia, Kara Mustafa Pasha's assault on Vienna, and John Milton's fall of Lucifer are all examples of leaders at the height of their power being undone when pride drives them to overreach the limits of their resources for victories that would have been prestigious but of questionable material and strategic value. They did not put the security and prosperity of the state above their own egos, a failure that echoes as loudly through history as any of their achievements.

Selfless leaders shape themselves to the demands of the position rather than forcing the system to adjust to their personalities and demands. All traits, abilities, and skills become tools for leaders to employ in service to the state. Paramount is the ability to know, for any given situation, what is required of them and the individuals they lead in order to accomplish the mission. Great leaders must develop judgment that relies first on information and second on the ability to translate information into action. Battlefield information is very important, but leaders must also have the background knowledge of what to do with that intelligence. They must also understand the motivations of their sailors and servicemen and how to best employ them; this is another kind of information, and acquiring it takes patience and diligence. Thousands of books, studies, and articles cover a vast field of knowledge applicable to us as U.S. Navy leaders. No one will ever be able to read and store all of this information. But it should be our constant quest to learn more, know more, and better apply that knowledge. Marcus Aurelius would have considered such study part of his duty as emperor. Our duty to our country does not end with our assigned tasks; we must be dedicated always to improving ourselves so that we may better serve our country.

Heroic models will never go away as a teaching tool. The Navy will never stop trying to define the qualities required to succeed, or figure out better ways to teach, instill, or bring out those qualities. It is our responsibility not just to mimic our predecessors, no matter how successful they were. We must under-stand the underlying reasons for their success. It is our duty to put aside the personal affinity we might feel toward any of these models and root out the principles on which we must each construct our own identity as leaders. The world could be filled with beautiful copies of St. Peter's Basilica, but wouldn't it be better filled with a thousand unique cathedrals all sharing the same principles of structural integrity?

Lieutenant League serves as the submarine-operations officer for Commander, Destroyer Squadron Seven. He conducted a historic home port shift to Singapore to serve as the operational commander for USS *Freedom* (LCS-1) and coordinate the CARAT series of bilateral exercises with regional partners. His previous assignments include electrical officer, chemical and radiological controls assistant, intel officer, and assistant operations on board the USS *North Carolina* (SSN-777).

20 "UNMANNED ETHICS"

ENS Samuel S. Lacinski, USN

Naval leadership ethics and professional military ethics require leaders to think about systems, platforms, and weapons as well as people. The spectrum of consideration is broad and the development and usage of unmanned aerial vehicles (UAVs) as well as unmanned ground, surface, and submersible vehicles in recent years require that naval leaders consider the political, moral, and military issues surrounding their use.

"UNMANNED ETHICS"

By ENS Samuel S. Lacinski, USN, U.S. Naval Institute *Proceedings* (September 2015): 34–38.

While drones are effective in combat, the political, moral, and military issues surrounding their use must be carefully considered.

The use of unmanned aerial vehicles (UAVs) has presented a complex and difficult array of dilemmas to military and political leadership. These systems bring a myriad of capabilities that are unavailable from other types of platforms. As the Navy pursues these technologies, understanding the ramifications of their employment in combat is critical. The fight against terrorists and insurgents over the course of the past decade-plus and the use of UAVs within these conflicts offer the Navy a valuable set of lessons from which to learn as it develops its own systems and doctrine. As the service sets its requirements for these systems, it must first consider their effectiveness. One of the most visible uses of UAVs has been their employment against asymmetric and non-state threats. With respect to the military, political, and ethical factors, UAVs are an effective and viable military technology in the targeting of non-state terrorist actors but present difficult considerations in their proper use.

Measuring Effectiveness

The first-order consideration for employing a given means to achieve a desired military objective should be the military effectiveness of that technology, defined here as the ability to inflict a desired consequence on an enemy combatant in the pursuit of desired objectives. The military effectiveness of UAVs is broken into three principal areas: the ability to gather persistent intelligence, the ability to effectively disrupt enemy capabilities and operations, and the ability to minimize collateral damage. With respect to intelligence gathering, UAVs are an ideally tailored platform for the demands of persistent surveillance. Originally designed for this role, the MQ-1 Predator and its larger, more advanced successor, the MQ-9 Reaper, are equipped with advanced sensor suites including an electro-optic/infrared sensor system with multiple spotting and view lenses. In addition, the aircraft can travel more than 400 nautical miles and loiter over a target in excess of 14 hours.[1] By merit of being unmanned, they are capable of staying airborne far longer than crewed aircraft and can fly into dangerous areas without risking an aircrew. The combination of these abilities presents a platform that is capable of reaching remote, difficult-to-access locales and providing video surveillance of those areas. UAVs have proven successful in this capacity in a variety of locations for more than a decade.[2]

Assessing the ability of UAVs to disrupt and degrade enemy capabilities requires analyzing their implementation in conflict. Examining the raw casualty figures as a result of UAV strikes provides a place to first assess their effect. The U.N. Special Rapporteur for Counter Terrorism and Human Rights (SRCT) Drone Inquiry estimated 1,600 combatants were killed in Pakistan by UAV strikes.[3] Viewing only combatants killed does not fully reflect the military value of using UAVs, however. By unleashing targeted attacks against key nodes in a terrorist organization, individual strikes can have far-reaching effects. The pressure applied by robust signal intelligence and persistent UAV surveillance combined with lethal and accurate strikes has forced al Qaeda and its affiliates to use slower forms of communications such as couriers to avoid interception, slowed the movements of these organizations to prevent detection, and hampered the ability to train for and carry out attacks.[4] Further, survivors of attacks spend time searching for possible informants, generating dissension within the groups.[5] Their appeals to the Pakistani government for a cessation of the strikes indicate their effect. Further, UAVs have proved effective at eliminating terrorist leadership including Tehrik-e-Taliban Pakistan founder Baitullah Mehsud; Islamic Movement of Uzbekistan leader Tahir Yuldashev; Majmiddin Jalolov, leader of the Islamic Jihad Union; and Saleh al-Somali, al Qaeda's chief of operations, among others.[6] The combination of these effects has produced a profound degradation on militant organizations that reduces their capabilities to launch regional and international attacks.

The final consideration in the military effectiveness of UAVs is their ability to reduce collateral damage, primarily reflected by the number of civilian casualties. The persistent surveillance capabilities of UAVs provide decision makers with a greater level of information when making targeting decisions. In addition, the weapon systems on board are highly accurate.[7] When combined with proper targeting protocols and decisions, the result is a high degree of precision in destroying only desired targets. Over the course of the entirety of UAV strikes in Pakistan, the SRCT report estimates 400 noncombatants were killed along with 200 additional "probable noncombatants."[8] This figure represents 27 percent of all casualties.[9] However, as the usage of UAVs evolved with improvements in intelligence, weapons, and stricter rules of engagement, civilian casualties were significantly reduced.[10] In nine strikes conducted in

Afghanistan thus far this year, an estimated one civilian has been killed relative to as many as 65 militants (1.5 percent of casualties).[11] UAVs, though imperfect, continue to make improvements in reducing collateral damage.

Weighing the Political Ramifications

Ceasing the analysis of the utility of UAVs at the simple tactical military advantage conferred by these systems would present an incomplete picture. An equally important consideration when conducting counterterrorism and counterinsurgency operations are the political consequences. While there are potentially significant domestic political concerns (consider the connotation of the word "drone" in the United States today), of greater import to military commanders are the political ramifications in theater, particularly from local populaces. UAV strikes in Pakistan, though conducted in coordination with Pakistani intelligence, have produced a degree of anti-American sentiment in the country.[12] David Kilcullen, an expert on counterinsurgency and an advisor to retired General David Petraeus, stated in May 2009 testimony before the House Armed Services Committee: "The drone strikes are highly unpopular, they are deeply aggravating the population. And they've given rise to a feeling of anger that coalesces the population around the extremists and leads to spikes of extremism."[13] A 2009 Gallup Pakistan poll found that only 9 percent of Pakistanis support the UAV strikes and 67 percent oppose.[14] Further, the failed airliner bombing over Detroit on 25 December 2009 and the failed Times Square bombing attempt on 1 May 2010 both cited UAV strikes as the motivation. This evidence suggests that UAVs are having a largely negative impact on the political and strategic objectives of the United States in the form of motivation for attacks and stoking anti-American sentiment.

However, this narrative is incomplete. Farhat Taj, a northwest Pakistan native currently working in Norway for the newspaper *The News*, claims, "Most of the literature misinforms in terms of civilian casualties caused by the attacks."[15] Based on conversations with locals of the Pakistani tribal areas where UAVs strike, she notes that many are actually in favor of the strikes, citing that they rid the locals of the "strictures, intimidation and violence associated with the Islamist militants living among them."[16] A 2008 study by the Aryana Institute for Regional Research and Advocacy found that of 550 professional people living in the tribal areas, about half characterized the strikes as "accurate," six in ten said the strikes were damaging to militant organizations, and a similar number denied they increased anti-Americanism sentiment.[17] The dichotomy of views and greater support from those directly affected by the strikes indicates that a more tangible sense for the security benefits of the strikes promotes a more favorable opinion of the activity. Further, the covert nature of the drone strikes and the subsequent dominance militant groups have over the flow of information result in a significant amount of disinformation and extremist propaganda influencing the perceptions of the populace.[18] On the whole, the use of UAVs for strikes produces negative reactions. However, the more acute reactions of those directly affected tend to be neutral or positive on balance. A more transparent campaign may push these views to areas beyond the strike theater.

Regardless of the military benefits and political ramifications, the United States should pursue ethical actions. When analyzing the morality of actions in war, Just War Theory provides the traditional framework. Just War Theory is broken into two principle elements, Jus ad Bellum, the ethical backing for going to war, and Jus in Bello, the ethical guidelines for the conduct of war.

Discrimination and Proportionality

Turning to the more obvious relationship between UAVs and Jus in Bello, for an act to be permissible in combat it must meet a series of requirements. Two requirements are particularly essential with respect to the use of UAVs: discrimination and proportionality. Discrimination requires that only military targets and combatants can be attacked. A military cannot legally directly target civilians. The second requirement, proportionality, requires that the military advantage gained by an attack cannot exceed the civilian damage.[19] As demonstrated previously, UAVs possess the technical capabilities to provide a high quantity of information to allow operators to make sound determinations between combatants and noncombatants when engaging targets. The precision weapon systems on board allow for accurate engagement of these targets. However, this technical precision does not guarantee accurate moral distinctions between legitimate and illegitimate targets.[20] A 2013 study by Lawrence Lewis, a researcher at the Center for Naval Analyses, indicated that UAV strikes were ten times more likely to cause civilian casualties per strike than those from manned platforms.

While the technical ability of UAVs and their weapon systems to hit their desired targets is clear, the ability of operators to select proper targets may be less so. To utilize the accuracy provided by UAV systems, operators must be highly competent in identifying proper targets and in recognizing and avoiding potential collateral damage. Better intelligence, particularly from sources on the ground, may improve the situational awareness of UAV operators and improve their ability to distinguish combatants from noncombatants. In addition, robust training is required to ensure that UAV operators have the same level of competency in recognizing combatants from noncombatants as manned aircraft pilots to ensure that recent reductions in civilian casualties are maintained.[21]

Proportionality requires weighing the anticipated military gain with the anticipated collateral damage. In counterterrorism and counterinsurgency, these two factors are inextricably linked. Collateral damage inherently reduces the military advantage conferred by a given action. As such, military planners maximize the value of a strike by minimizing the collateral damage. Satisfying the proportionality constraint will vary from strike to strike, as the target that is being engaged and its perceived value will have vastly different "acceptable levels" of collateral damage. The tolerated risk to civilians for a strike on a single, lone Taliban rifleman would be significantly different than the level tolerated to kill ISIS leader Abu Bakr al-Baghdadi. Michael Walzer, a leading philosopher on Just War Theory, contends that "even if the target is very important and the number of innocent people threatened relatively small, [military planners] must risk soldiers before they kill civilians."[22] However, Asa Kasher, an Israeli philosopher and linguist, and Amos Yaldin, former head of the Israel Defense Forces Intelligence Directorate, argue against this position, contending that terrorists excuse military combatants from this responsibility by intermingling with noncombatants.[23]

This consideration should not be lost on commanders, though. Minimizing risk to one's own forces can serve in opposition to the intended objectives. As the counterinsurgency manual states, "If military forces remain in their compounds, they lose touch with the people, appear to be running scared, and cede the initiative to the insurgents."[24] This is particularly true with UAV strikes in remote areas where ground forces are not routinely present and engaged with the populace. As a general rule, to satisfy the proportionality criteria, commanders should work to minimize collateral damage to the greatest extent possible. If an option exists that incurs an increased risk to soldiers but a decreased risk to civilians, this is the option the commander should execute. UAVs can satisfy the proportionality constraint and in many circumstances present the best possible means to do so. However, commanders need to remain keenly aware that the technical capabilities and perceptions of precision surrounding UAVs do not exonerate them from "the determination of legal or ethical legitimacy."[25]

Hostage Deaths Emphasize the High Stakes

The recent tragic deaths of two al Qaeda hostages, American Warren Weinstein and Italian Giovanni Lo Porto, highlight the need for consistent and vigilant caution in conducting UAV strikes. Weinstein and Lo Porto were killed in a CIA strike in the Shawal Valley, Pakistan, conducted in January, despite persistent surveillance by UAVs for hundreds of hours.[26] In the wake of such failures, keeping a strategic view of the overall situation is imperative. As President Barack Obama said in his statement regarding the deaths, "It is a cruel and bitter truth that in the fog of war generally and our fight against terrorists specifically, mistakes, sometimes deadly mistakes, can occur."[27] Even the most cautious, well-intentioned measures will not prevent all unintended consequences of an action. Due to the extensive surveillance of the target, it is unlikely that another platform, outside of direct action by "boots on the ground," would have prevented the deaths of the hostages. It is also important to note that, despite the deaths, UAVs are still "the least costly means of eliminating militants whose first aim is to kill Americans."[28]

However, specific improvements in the operational methodology of the UAV program may help prevent such situations in the future. First, the control of lethal UAV strikes should be transferred from the CIA to the U.S. military. Doing so would allow for a greater level of transparency as the military can report on its actions. This may create a more challenging diplomatic environment for conducting strikes, particularly in Pakistan.[29] However, military control is necessary not only to ensure the proper conduct of operators in the future but also to allow for a more robust effort to engage locals and provide a more positive narrative surrounding the campaign.

On balance, the totality of UAVs' performance in the nation's 21st century conflicts indicates their ability as a capable and valuable asset. UAVs present military commanders and political leaders with an asset capable of persistent surveillance with the ability to conduct precise strikes over dangerous and difficult-to-access locales. These capabilities have been successfully demonstrated over the course of the past decade in conflict against militants in various settings around the world. In addition, the application of these systems has improved during their usage, with noted improvements being observed in civilian casualty rates in recent years. However, for the United States to be able to fully leverage the advantages conferred by these capabilities, it would be wise to better illuminate the campaign. Doing so would shed light on the legality and moral authority of the practices in place to the international community while also preventing the alienation of populaces affected by these strikes. Finally, operators and commanders must continue to improve on their abilities to make difficult moral determinations when employing UAVs to ensure their continued effectiveness on the battlefield within the bounds of Just War. As the Navy moves to develop and employ its own UAV fleet, it would be wise to reflect on and learn from the lessons of the previous conflicts. Doing so will allow for a better equipped system with more prepared operators for the range of threats that will be encountered.

Ensign Lacinski is a 2015 graduate of the U.S. Naval Academy and selected naval aviation. Prior to reporting to flight school, he is pursuing a master's of science degree in aerospace engineering and technology and policy at the Massachusetts Institute of Technology.

Notes

1. Ryan L. Brown and Brian G. Smith, "Technical elegance vs. political conse-
    quence," *The SciTech Lawyer* 7.1: 24 (2010).
2. Dave Sloggett, "Attack of the drones—The utility of UAVs in fighting terror-
    ism," *Jane's Intelligence Review*, 16 July 2010, https://janes.ihs.com/.
3. United Nations Human Rights, "UN SRCT Drone Inquiry," http://unsrct-
    drones.com/report/63.
4. Sloggett, "Attack of the drones."
5. Scott Shane, "C.I.A. to Expand Use of Drones in Pakistan," *New York Times*,
    4 December 2009, www.nytimes.com/2009/12/04/world/asia/04drones.
    html?pagewanted=all.
6. Sloggett, "Attack of the drones."
7. Sarah Kreps and John Kaag, "The Use of Unmanned Aerial Vehicles in Con-
    temporary Conflict: A Legal and Ethical Analysis," *Polity* 44, no. 2 (April 2012):
    260–285.
8. "UN SRCT Drone Inquiry."
9. Carl Conetta, "The Wages of War: Iraqi Combatant and Noncombatant Fatali-
    ties in the 2003 Conflict," Project on Defense Alternatives, www.comw.org/
    pda/0310rm8ap2.html#1.
10. Sloggett, "Attack of the drones."
11. "Get the data: Drone Wars, Casualty estimates," The Bureau of Investiga-
    tive Journalism, www.thebureauinvestigates.com/category/projects/drones/
    drones-graphs/.
12. Shane, "C.I.A. to Expand Use."
13. Brown and Smith, "Technical elegance."
14. Shane, "C.I.A. to Expand Use."
15. Sloggett, "Attack of the drones.
16. Ibid.
17. Shane, "C.I.A. to Expand Use."
18. Sloggett, "Attack of the drones."
19. Linda Johansson, "Is it morally right to use unmanned aerial vehicles (UAVs)
    in war?" *Philosophy & Technology* 24.3 (2011).
20. Kreps, Kaag, "Use of Unmanned Aerial Vehicles."
21. Lawrence Lewis, "Drone Strikes: Civilian Casualty Considerations," *Center for
    Naval Analyses*, June 2013.
22. Kreps and Kaag, "Use of Unmanned Aerial Vehicles."
23. Ibid.
24. Ibid.

25. Ibid.

26. Craig Whitlock, Missy Ryan, and Greg Miller, "Obama apologizes for attack that killed two hostages," *Washington Post*, 23 April 2015.

27. Ibid.

28. "Drone strikes are bad; no drone strikes would be worse," *Washington Post*, 1 May 2015.

29. Ibid.

21 "THE DEBATE ON ETHICS MUST CONTINUE"

Gen Charles C. Krulak, USMC (Ret.)

Taking as its touchstone the teaching of leadership and ethics at the Naval Academy, the following essay by former Commandant of the United States Marine Corps General Charles C. Krulak calls for a "holistic approach to the complete area of leadership, character development, and ethics." He calls for selfless leadership and integrity from men and women who know their profession and treat those they lead with dignity and respect. Such leadership builds upon but moves beyond the classroom and strengthens not only the individual, but also, the profession of arms.

"THE DEBATE ON ETHICS MUST CONTINUE"

By Gen Charles C. Krulak, USMC, U.S. Naval Institute *Proceedings* (December 2000): 96.

Over the past year, articles have been published, e-mails disseminated, speeches given, and discussions conducted on character development/leadership/ethics instruction at the U.S. Naval Academy. For better or worse, I have been associated with a portion of the ongoing debate. With that in mind, I thought it might be worthwhile to share the central thesis I have regarding our character development/leadership/ethics program.

I do not believe we have captured the balance that is needed to provide the young men and women at the Naval Academy with the type of experiences, both classroom and real-world, that will help make them successful on the battlefields of the 21st century. Because these battlefields will be chaotic, our future leaders need to know and understand that there is a philosophy associated with the profession of arms that is found not in the minds of classical thinkers but, rather, in the blood, sweat, and tears of naval officers who have succeeded on past battlefields.

Like my friend and classmate, Bernie McGuire, I attended ethics classes at the Naval Academy. I went unannounced because I wanted to see things without the normal "spin" that comes from a visit prompted by an invitation. To be fair, my visits were more than a year ago—a completely different academic year—and I am sure much has changed since then. At the same time, what I saw was a disconnect between theory and reality. When I talked off-line to the midshipmen, they expressed concern that they were not getting enough reality. More important, I had naval officers (instructors) tell me the same thing.

I know about the leadership challenges of war and peace, and I know that what brings success is not an understanding of Kantian ethics. Rather, it is good, old-fashioned leadership that is fostered by great examples (living and dead) and experiences generated by a knowledgeable faculty and an Academy that allows freedom to fail but ensures accountability and, therefore, allows learning to occur. Isn't that what we all want? Isn't that what our Nation deserves?

Contrary to Bernie McGuire's observations published in a recent issue of the Naval Academy Alumni Association's *Shipmate* magazine, I did not find the learning dynamic to be much different from what my classmates and I experienced when we attended the Naval Academy in the early 1960s. The professors made the classes, not the students. When the professors truly taught, the mids responded with their ideas, thoughts, and energy; when the professors failed to teach, the mids responded accordingly. Not much has changed.

Without questioning why the problem ever existed, I applaud the fact that the Naval Academy has corrected it, identified by Bernie McGuire and highlighted by midshipmen and instructors, with Navy and Marine officers teaching philosophy and civilians teaching operational context. The Superintendent, Vice Admiral John Ryan, has been quite willing to make changes where needed, and he certainly deserves kudos for that.

With respect to the NE-203 ethics class, that single course has gained far too much attention and has obscured the real issues. Suffice it to say that the Naval Academy only has a finite amount of time to teach leadership/character development to our future officers, and every class should be evaluated to determine the value added based on instructor time available. I am sure the Naval Academy's leadership is doing that type of evaluation, and NE-203 is part of that evaluation.

With respect to the issue of today's environment—gender, race, and religious differences—which supposedly makes educating and training midshipmen more difficult than in years past, it is a red herring. Each generation brings its own baggage, but the basic tenets of leadership have not changed over the ages: Be men and women of character; know your stuff; take care of your people; treat each person with respect and dignity; be men and women of integrity; and be selfless.

We need to teach our midshipmen these immutable concepts. We need to put them into a context that every young man and woman can easily recognize and identify with, as being part of the profession of arms. We need to hold the midshipmen accountable at the Naval Academy and, when they are commissioned, in the Fleet. What is truly needed is a holistic approach to the complete area of leadership, character development, and ethics. That is all I am saying—and all I have ever said.

Having spent 36 years dealing with several generations of young men and women, the one thing I am dead certain about is that today's youth are not that different from us. They want to do something of value, to make a difference, to be given a goal to shoot for, to be given responsibility, and then to be held accountable for that responsibility. We just need to feed them the opportunities.

If we challenge them, are honest with them, do not send mixed signals to them, and are willing to admit when we are wrong, we will bring the best out of these talented people.

What is important is that the issue of leadership, character development, and ethics continues to be studied and debated. We owe it to these midshipmen, the Navy-Marine Corps team, and the nation to get it right.

An infantry officer, **General Krulak** served in the Corps from 1964 to 1999.

22 "LETTER TO MY SON"

Anonymous

Written in the 1950s by the CO of a cruiser to his son who was approaching graduation from the Naval Academy and commissioning, this letter might just as easily have been written to any young officer commencing service in the naval profession of arms. Drawing upon his own experiences and more than a quarter century of service, the captain affirms that "the naval profession has no superior in honor and service to its country." Yet those who enter it must often balance competing demands of time, expertise, energies, and resources in a complex technical and operational environment. At the foundation of this is what the author terms the "moral fiber" of the individual and he encourages the soon-to-be officer to "never lose sight of the individual in our profession." Military professionalism rests on the foundation of individual character and integrity.

"LETTER TO MY SON"

By Anonymous, U.S. Naval Institute *Proceedings*
(December 1955): 310–13.

21 May 1955

Dear Son,

A little over a quarter of a century ago I was on the verge, as you are today, of being graduated from the Naval Academy. No doubt your thoughts now, as mine were then, are occupied largely with the imminent release from a rigid routine of studies, drills, classes and a restriction of liberties that few people undergo for such an extended period. It is right and proper that you should anticipate this release, because it, together with the honor that comes with graduation, is a reward for which you can well be proud.

It is only natural that on this occasion I should reflect upon the years that have passed since I stood in your present position, and recall some of the lessons that they have brought. Also, it is perhaps only natural that I should want to pass those lessons along to you with the hope that they will be of some benefit to you in your career. For, in order that man progress, isn't it necessary that each generation build upon the experiences of those that have gone before?

In reality these thoughts that I pass along for your consideration are not new but, rather, are well proven truths that are brought more sharply into focus with the passing of time. They are frequently either forgotten or disregarded by many who would readily recognize their worth, but who find the press of everyday living too exacting to give them the attention they deserve.

The naval profession has no superior in honor and service to its country. It has played a major role in the establishment and maintenance of virtually all great nations, and particularly our own. It is a profession that is respected, trusted, and depended upon by the civilian populace. It could not have reached its present stature and survived so long had it not yielded returns commensurate with the country's investment and faith in it. There-fore, the uniform is one we wear with a pride that raises it above any act of dishonor.

Periodically there are those who maintain that the Navy is outmoded, and that wars can be fought and won more quickly and cheaply without a major naval effort. One of the greatest mistakes that the United States could make would be to succumb to such a philosophy. To do so would be to voluntarily sacrifice one of the major elements of a strategical and tacti-cal combination of air force, army, and naval forces that, when employed in concert, are far stronger than the sum of their separate strengths. Periods of naval ultra-conservatism have been left far behind. The Navy of today, and of recent decades, has incorporated the use of the most modern weap-ons and equipments. Virtually the entire range of modern technological advancements has multiplied the Navy's striking power many-fold, and we are well embarked upon further strides forward. I am not alone in forecast-ing naval developments in the near future that will dwarf anything that we have seen in the past. Nuclear power, nuclear weapons, electronics, and guided missiles are present day realities, but still in their infancy. You are most fortunate in entering the Navy at a time when you can participate in such development and growth.

Modern technology and its adaptation to military uses receive much publicity, attention, and stress. They are rightfully sources of pride. Regard-less, however, of the importance of scientific achievement the prime ingre-dient of our profession is the human being, the individual. We call many of our weapons and equipment automatic. They are not automatic. Some-where along the line their input and, consequently, their output are prod-ucts of the human mind.

We must never lose sight of the importance of the individual in our profession, regardless of any apparently humble part he plays. Our weapons become progressively more destructive, and our equipments more efficient, but at the same time they both become more complicated. The time required for training the operating and maintenance personnel is likewise becoming progressively longer. The chances for error on the part of some individual in the chain of control become progressively greater. Every man of every rate must be constantly alert to do the right thing at the right time, and he must know of his importance and the heavy responsibility that he carries. I have found that a man's sentiments, emotions, and personal feelings are not dependent upon his rate or rank. The basic superiority of democracy lies in its emphasis upon recognition of the individual human being.

Many things combine to submerge the individual in modem living. In both civilian and military life people are all too frequently dealt with in masses and classes in an impersonal manner. In the Armed Services they are frequently known better by their written service record than they are personally by those in whose hands lies their destiny. The very bigness of our Navy and the many and varied duties of the higher ranking officers militate against that close personal association which is so desirable.

Actually, the Navy is well organized to retain many of the advantages of a small organization, even though it, as a service, is large. The personnel of ships and stations are divided up into comparatively small units of divisions. These are normally in charge of an officer who is in an excellent position to know each man individually and to exercise and develop a high degree of leadership. Those years while you are a division officer or a junior division officer afford an outstanding opportunity for you to further develop and exercise leadership.

I have seen officers and men repeatedly spend many consecutive hours of daylight and darkness repairing defective equipment. When the need arises we must make a comparable effort on behalf of a man who has erred. We should be able to detect quickly those erring individuals who will benefit from our guidance, and we must turn to in their behalf with even more zeal than with a piece of defective equipment.

The American youth is wonderful material with which to work. He usually comes to the Navy while young and still in his formative years. Aside from his technical training his value to the Navy depends greatly upon what we call "moral fiber." The decline of many nations, ancient, medieval, and modern, can be attributed to the loss of the moral fiber of their citizenry. American greatness can never survive its loss.

What do I mean by the term "moral fiber"? I cannot hope to define it completely. In itself it is somewhat intangible, but its manifestations are readily apparent when crises arise. We might say it consists of such things as honor, integrity, self-respect, fortitude in adversity, and the will to win. These are some of the things that have been implanted in the average American youth by the average American home, church, and school. Fostering and encouraging their growth while these men are in our charge is a heavy responsibility that we must never forget nor fail to accept.

This philosophy of stressing the importance of the individual does not incorporate in any sense a doctrine of undue softness. Tautness and firmness in a leader, when administered with justice, will generate respect and inspire subordinates, whereas softness will undermine morale quickly.

I mentioned earlier the relaxation that will accompany the release from the rigid program that you have followed for the past four years. The change will be a radical one. While you will continue to meet schedules and adhere to prescribed routines you will have a great deal more freedom. This freedom is not limited to a physical sense only, but is extended to include many aspects of the performance of your duties. In other words, you will not be told in such detail as to how to do many things, and your own initiative will be allowed to display itself to a far greater extent than heretofore. Many are slow to make this transformation. They accept the freedom but do not shoulder readily the responsibilities that come with it. I suggest that you recognize the possibilities of such an error and that you enter into your new duties as an officer with enthusiasm and energy without delay. I have seen many young officers take too long to make a start, and the longer one waits the harder it becomes. Time does not permit delay. Your career will rush by at an incredible speed. Each new job will bring with it increased responsibilities that can be discharged best only if full advantage has been taken of the time and experiences that have gone before.

Some may feel that the Navy makes demands upon us that are beyond the capacity of the average individual. I do not agree. The difference between superiority and mediocrity in performance is more often the result of the difference between application of the talents we have rather than because of the lack of inherent ability.

As regards motivation I would rule out the immediate objective of pleasing your seniors as an end in itself. In this regard I can do no better than to pass on advice that I received when I was first graduated. It was to the effect that each assignment should be carried out to the very best of my ability, and with a pride of accomplishment rather than a hope of reward as a major motivation.

I think it important that all officers reflect occasionally upon the basic nature of a naval career as compared to most civilian professions. We are the servants of a benevolent country, and our motivation stems more from devotion to service than from materialistic rewards. Historically, nations pass through dynamic and passive phases. The United States at the present time is in a dynamic phase requiring the highest caliber of public servants, of which class the military is a part. In my opinion it is unfortunate that this phase should be accompanied by such heavy emphasis upon national and individual materialism. An *esprit de corps* based upon a love of service and country must take precedence over materialism as the philosophy of naval officers.

The above is not intended to infer that a naval career does not offer some materialistic rewards. A close analysis of the salary and security features will disclose many advantages of a naval career from the financial security point of view. However, these advantages more normally accrue to those who spend most of their life, rather than only a few years, in the service. In reality, the financial rewards can be considerably enhanced by exercising a greater degree of individual frugality than most of us do. Except in those rare instances of unavoidable financial adversity I think it possible and appropriate that officers of all ranks set aside a portion of their salary as savings.

We must resist any tendency to be stifled in personal progress by confining our efforts to routine duties. Advantage should be taken of spare time to expand our knowledge of history, strategy, tactics, and comparable items that touch on our profession. There is much along these lines to absorb, and habits for such study should be begun at the outset of your career and cultivated assiduously. U.S. naval history and tradition are particularly inspiring and they deserve more attention and study than given by the average naval officer. When the fury of the Battle of Pearl Harbor broke upon us unexpectedly we were reduced largely to individual, or small group, action. I was surprised to note flashing through my mind thoughts of our rich naval heritage, and such thoughts provided further incentives for any efforts on my part that day, modest as they were.

The naval profession has many interesting aspects that make it a highly desirable profession. However, it is not all glamour. Like virtually all professions it contains much detailed work that, considered in itself, could be called drudgery. Records, figures, curves, and statistics require tedious work but they serve as bases for very important decisions. Their compilation must receive the same conscientious effort as the more glamorous aspects of your work.

Your career will be unusual if it does not include disappointments, frustrations, and discouragement. These may at times appear to be overwhelming, but they must not be allowed to persist. One of the standards by which men are measured is the extent to which they overcome adversity.

You will, no doubt, encounter considerable internal criticism of Navy procedures in various fields. Most of us will readily admit that room exists for improvement, but it cannot be accomplished solely by verbal criticism. Furthermore, initiation of action for improvement is, primarily, the responsibility of those of us within the Navy, rather than of those without. All ranks and ratings should therefore be constantly on the alert for detecting the need for such action. A word of caution is appropriate here. Custom, precedent, and protocol sometimes stand in the way of action that might appear desirable. Should there be a question that the proposed action might violate these, or official regulations, your seniors should be consulted before taking flights into the unknown. A large portion of your proposals may be thereby stopped short of implementation, but don't be too discouraged. After all, it is better to have one's wings clipped rather than atrophied by disuse.

The average naval officer may appear to possess a self-sufficient and independent air that exhibits little need for reliance upon Divine assistance and guidance. Do not trust such an impression. I have found that, in the majority of the naval officers of my acquaintance, there is a devotion to God that belies a seemingly hard exterior. Such devotion is usually, and quite appropriately, quiet and unostentatious but it is a unique source of strength. Thanks to the Divinity in times of triumph, reliance upon His guidance when faced with a difficult decision, and a request for His assistance in the midst of adversity are not unmasculine acts.

The serious vein of this letter up to this point might leave the impression that little room is left in the naval profession for relaxation and recreation, and that it is too exacting to be enjoyed. If such an impression has been left I want to dispel it completely. I think there is no better way to close this letter than to assure you that much joy and pleasure are inherent in the profession itself. Retain your cheerful nature, your sense of humor, your zest for living. They will stand you in good stead, and you will find ample outlets for them all. Cultivate friendships, both service and civilian; pursue cultural interests; broaden your horizons constantly. The environment is favorable for these accomplishments. Exploit it fully and your contentment will enhance your value to the Navy, your country, and yourself.

Welcome aboard,
Dad

This article in its present form was, in fact, a letter written by the commanding officer of a cruiser to his son on the occasion of his son's graduation from the U.S. Naval Academy in June, 1955. It came to the attention of the Board of Control of the U.S. Naval Institute and, because of the intrinsic worth of its sound advice, is shared here with our members.

23 "LEADERSHIP LESSONS FROM THE HANOI HILTON"

Peter Fretwell and Taylor Baldwin Kiland

The legacy of Vice Admiral James B. Stockdale is a solid link in the chain of U.S. Navy history. His leadership as a POW in Vietnam embodied naval leadership ethics and leadership in the profession of arms. He and other POWs endured isolation, deprivation, and torture but returned with honor. The Hoa Lo Camp, Hanoi, better known as the "Hanoi Hilton," was a forge for then-present and future leaders. Beyond the extraordinary stories of the survival of the POWs, the authors glean from the experiences of the POWs' leadership lessons that are applicable in any command.

"LEADERSHIP LESSONS FROM THE HANOI HILTON"

By Peter Fretwell and Taylor Baldwin Kiland, U.S. Naval Institute *Proceedings* (November 2009): 64–68.

Vice Admiral James Stockdale's principles can inspire any organization's leaders.

The USS *Stockdale* (DDG-106) was commissioned in April 2009 in Santa Barbara, California. The man for whom the destroyer is named, Vice Admiral James

Bond Stockdale, left the U.S. Navy an inspiring legacy. During the Vietnam War, he was the senior ranking prisoner-of-war officer at the Hoa Lo Camp, Hanoi, better known as the Hanoi Hilton.

Then-Commander Stockdale was a devotee of Epictetus, the eminent Greek philosopher. Stockdale had admired him since studying Stoic philosophy at Stanford University, from which he earned a master's degree in International Relations and Marxist Theory in 1962. Epictetus' Stoicism is the key to understanding Stockdale's character, focus, and determination. His later writings and speeches frequently cited the Stoic philosopher as he sought to explain his success as the leader of the POW population in the Hanoi Hilton for more than seven years (1965–73).

From POWs to National Leaders

The Hanoi Hilton POWs were an unusual and remarkable group. Instead of returning home unraveled from years of abuse, isolation, and deprivation, about 80 percent of the 591 men that Operation Homecoming returned continued their military service. Many later became leaders in government, business, law, or academia. Twenty-four attained the rank of admiral or general; 18 have served (or are serving) in elected or appointed political positions at both the federal and state levels, including as senators, U.S. representatives, Federal Trade Commissioner, and the first U.S. Ambassador to the Socialist Republic of Vietnam. Numerous others served in executive positions in corporate America and small business; many also continue to serve in their local communities for scouting, religious, and civic organizations. Eight received the Medal of Honor.

Despite being the longest-held group of POWs in our nation's history, they brought home most of their comrades without major incidents of long-term mental illness. According to the Robert E. Mitchell Center for Prisoner of War Studies in Pensacola, Florida, 96 percent of the Hanoi Hilton POWs were free of post-traumatic stress disorder. By comparison, a 1997 American Psychiatric Association report found more than half of 262 World War II and Korean War POWs studied had symptoms of lifetime PTSD.

The book *Open Doors: Vietnam POWs Thirty Years Later* (by Taylor Kiland and Jamie Howren, Potomac Books, 2005) made use of 30 interviews as well as studies analyzing physical and mental health over the past 35 years. This research revealed key (and rare) leadership traits that surfaced in the Hanoi Hilton during the 1960s and early 1970s. Stockdale developed many specific leadership philosophies while in captivity, but in an overarching sense he understood the need for three conditions if the POWs were to succeed:

Invisible leadership: Unit cohesion had to be maintained, as did adherence to principles and inspiration of the men—with no visual or verbal contact with subordinates. Military discipline and the code of conduct alone could not accomplish this. Communication strategies had to be developed to overcome the forced isolation. Stockdale's leadership philosophy, as guided by Epictetus and the Stoics, can serve as a model for managing and influencing dispersed or virtual teams.

Strong cultural norms: The organizational culture had to be infectious; it had to spread on its own. Today we call this viral culture. More than 700 POWs in North Vietnam were separated by walls and spread across geographically dispersed prison camps. Stockdale needed to create and aim for consistent goals that could be sustained for years, if necessary.

He and the other POWs succeeded in maintaining operations under severely restrictive conditions for five to eight years. The cultural "norms" that they developed—unit cohesion, cultural consistency, focus in the face of physical and organizational barriers—can apply to business and organizational leadership anywhere.

Keeping the faith: The POWs needed to keep their perspective amid isolation, deprivation, and torture. In this regard, attitude played a major role in improving morale and ensuring survival. Some of the most severely wounded prisoners healed; indeed, it was not the degree of injury that determined death or survival. On the contrary, the POWs maintain that attitude was the key factor. Humility and perspective were critical factors in providing the motivation for keeping the faith.

Wall Tap Society

Stockdale provided the leadership to inspire the men in his chain of command. Tactically, he used the tap code and other clandestine communications methods to achieve this. He conceived and conveyed his motivational messages even while in solitary confinement.

Stockdale's genius emerged in startling ways, many of which are well documented. Jim Collins' management book *Good to Great* (New York: Harper-Collins, 2001) covers some of Stockdale's philosophies and techniques. The code that he and his fellow POWs created to communicate through prison walls was a clever method, but he also used the tool to establish his leadership position, exercise his authority, and inspire his men, many of whom he had never met.

He describes their collective organizational mission in his essay *Courage Under Fire: Testing Epictetus's Doctrines in a Laboratory of Human Behavior* (Hoover Institution on War Revolution and Peace, Stanford University, 1998):

> We organized a clandestine society via our wall tap code, a society with our own laws, traditions, customs, even heroes. [This explains how we could] . . . order each other into more torture . . . refuse to comply with specific demands, intentionally call the bluff of our jailers and in a real sense force them to repeat the full ropes process to another submission. . . . At least half of those wonderful competitive fly-boys I found myself locked up with [said things like]: "We are in a spot like we've never been in before. But we deserve to maintain our self-respect, to have the feeling we are fighting back. We can't refuse to do every degrading thing they demand of us, but it's up to you, boss, to pick out the things we must all refuse to do unless and until they put us through the ropes again. . . . Give us the list; what are we to take torture for?"

Stockdale was faced with a Gordian Knot:

> I put a lot of thought into what those first orders should be. . . . My mind-set was "we here under the gun are the experts . . . throw out the

book and write your own." My orders came out as easy-to-remember acronyms. The principal one was BACK-US: Don't Bow in public; stay off the Air; admit no Crimes, never Kiss them goodbye. "US" could be interpreted as United States, but it really meant "Unity over Self" (pp. 14–15).

One for All

By carefully choosing a few simple principles that most POWs could embrace, Stockdale set the ground rules for a culture that could be self-guiding and self-perpetuating. He set goals that were in the men's own self-interest as well as in that of everyone else. Stockdale understood that he was forced to rely on others to live by the principles without being micromanaged.

Because of the harsh reality of his environment, this hands-off approach was a necessity. He knew he had to inspire, not dictate. Outside of society's comforts and freedom, humility reigned and improvisation was the norm. Stockdale laid down a code that was firm enough to guide but flexible enough to allow for innovation. This was his brilliance.

Today, situational-leadership theory preaches what Stockdale practiced: leaders must change their style to fit the environment and their followers' needs and skills. Any organization that articulates a purposeful goal in front of its members has started building a culture in which individuality can support solidarity, and in which personal desires (especially those of top management) take a backseat to the common good.

All for One

Stockdale frequently emphasized that every POW held different values and views on life, and that this diversity was an attribute. Each was his own man. Their memoirs—Howard Rutledge's *In the Presence of Mine Enemies,* Jeremiah Denton Jr.'s *When Hell Was In Session,* George Day's *Return with Honor,* Robinson Risner's *Passing of the Night,* James A. Mulligan's *Hanoi Commitment,* Sam Johnson's *Captive Warriors,* John Dramesi's *Code of Honor,* and Larry Guarino's *POW's Story: 2801 Days in Hanoi,* and more—show how differently they saw their plight, their own actions, and one another. The POWs were not a case study in conformity. Knowing this, Stockdale harnessed the diversity and gave them latitude. And in their common purpose, he also held out hope and solidarity.

Orson Swindle wrote in a 2005 issue of *Proceedings*:

One day we young officers were discussing some issue and finding no answers. I whispered down the passageway, "Hang on for a minute, and let me ask the Old Man what we should do." Commander Stockdale came up after a couple of calls, and responded with a wise answer to our problem.

Now fast forward to February 1973, almost six years later. We have been told we are going home. In the large courtyard area of Ho Loa prison [the Hanoi Hilton], the North Vietnamese are allowing one large cell of Americans at a time to wander over to the recently uncovered windows of other cells that surrounded the courtyard, permitting conversation. I see a slight man, terribly worn and tired looking with very grey hair limping over to my window. He looks up at me, smiles, and says, "Hi, I'm Jim Stockdale, who are you?" We literally had never seen each other before ("Always Leading and Always Will," U.S. Naval Institute *Proceedings*, August 2005, p. 65).

Instincts and Perspective

Most POWs cite training and the military's Code of Conduct to explain their initial behavior after capture. They drew on the military bearing that had been drilled into them during boot camp or officer training, the rote adherence to procedures ingrained in pilots, and the austere "name, rank, serial number, date of birth" required by the Code. But for most, this rigor helped only in the immediate aftermath of capture.

Respect for and adherence to a well-defined chain of command also provided boundaries, rules, and a built-in operational procedure. However, a chain of command does not ingrain principles or inspire men. What neither it nor the code of conduct can easily explain is the consistency of the culture that evolved and was adopted by the highly dispersed and disparate individuals who were part of Stockdale's wall-tap society for many years. They were members of the intensely mission-focused, unity-driven organization that Stockdale described: BACK-US.

In assembling his core leadership at the Hanoi Hilton, Stockdale looked beyond rank. In *Courage Under Fire*, Stockdale advises: "When instincts and rank are out of phase, take the guy with the instincts." He understood that attitude often accounts for an outcome more than do skills or background.

In more than 1,300 inspirational speeches, former POW Commander Paul Galanti has summarized his perspective on daily life after the Hanoi Hilton: "There's no such thing as a bad day when you have a door knob on the inside of the door."

Your Brother's Keeper

Admiral Stockdale was able to keep the perspective of his charges uppermost in his mind during the grueling years in the Hanoi Hilton. He did it by deciding deliberately, with the conscious intent of a great leader, to shoulder the responsibility of using wisely whatever power accrued to his position as the senior ranking officer of the POWs.

Stockdale practiced "servant leadership," the belief that leaders should prioritize the needs of followers, long before it was popularized in business circles. He wrote in *Thoughts of a Philosophical Fighter Pilot* (Hoover Institution Press, Stanford University, 1995): "A leader must remember he is responsible for his charges. He must tend his flock, not only cracking the whip but 'washing their feet' when they are in need of help." The approach frees the flock to look out for each other and the greater good.

In a 1981 address to the graduating class of John Carroll University, Stockdale encapsulated his POW leadership: "From this eight-year experience, I distilled one all-purpose idea. . . . It is a simple idea . . . an idea that naturally and spontaneously comes to men under pressure. . . . You are your brother's keeper."

Mr. Fretwell, general manager of the Classical Network in New Jersey, holds an MBA in strategic leadership. He has widely studied Stockdale's writings on leadership in the Hanoi Hilton.

Ms. Kiland, vice-president of marketing communications at the United States Navy Memorial, Washington, D.C., holds an MS in integrated marketing communications. A former naval officer, she is the author or co-author of several books.

24 "LESSONS IN STOIC LEADERSHIP"

ENS Jesse Burroughs, USN

Members of the naval profession have many sources from which to draw for lessons, illustrations, and reflections in leadership and professional ethics. Among these is the example of Vice Admiral James Bond Stockdale whose leadership as a prisoner of war in Vietnam was recognized with the Congressional Medal of Honor. Admiral Stockdale often wrote and spoke of his intellectual indebtedness to the Stoic philosopher Epictetus. In the following essay the author presents aspects of Stoicism that he believes are relevant to the military leader and profession of arms, illustrating them from the captivity of Admiral Stockdale.

"LESSONS IN STOIC LEADERSHIP"

By ENS Jesse Burroughs, USN, U.S. Naval Institute *Proceedings* (December 2014): 66–70.

2014 Leadership Essay Contest Winner

When developing their character, junior officers should look to naval leaders who embraced the philosophy of Stoicism.

Vice Admiral James Stockdale is a naval legend and an American hero. A U.S. Naval Academy graduate renowned for his leadership capability as well as his fortitude and courage as a prisoner of war, Stockdale is an example of leadership for many young naval officers. His leadership principles rest on the foundations of Stoicism as set forth by the Roman philosopher Epictetus. While it is unlikely that most naval officers will experience the hardships of being a prisoner of war, the concepts of Stoicism can be applied to everyday leadership in practical ways. In fact, military leadership calls for Stoic leadership, as a naval officer cannot let emotions influence actions. An officer must follow all legal orders to the best of his or her ability whether in agreement or not, ensuring the moral course is taken. If the principles of Stoicism worked for Vice Admiral Stockdale while he was prisoner of war then these same principles will benefit naval officers in all leadership roles.

Leadership is complex and difficult, which is illustrated by the thousands of classes, books, and seminars that focus on the subject. Numerous theories exist on leadership, and countless styles abound, with a correspondingly high number of definitions. The *Oxford English Dictionary* defines it as "the action of leading a group or organization." However, this simple definition does not encapsulate the true nature of leadership. Difficult to define, the quality is much easier to recognize, especially in individuals.

The history of naval services provides many excellent examples of leadership, such as Medal of Honor recipients Vice Admiral Stockdale and Lieutenant Michael Murphy, as well as Captain David Marquet of the USS *Santa Fe* (SSN-763), and Captain Paul X. Rinn of the USS *Samuel B. Roberts* (FFG-58). All these men exhibited signs of Stoic leadership, accepting in the face of impossible odds what they could and could not control—in other words, the external and the internal.

An Issue of Character

The basis of Stoicism is the development of character and self-discipline to overcome destructive emotions. What lies beyond our control is the external, such as the actions of other people, events, and reputation. What lies in our control is the internal, such as our own opinions, actions, and desires. Recognizing the external and internal is the first step in Stoic leadership.

The continued development of character is essential in Stoic leadership. In a speech to the University of London, Stockdale quoted Epictetus, noting "You must labor to improve either your own governing principles or externals, you must work hard either on the inner man, or the things outside; that is, play the role of a philosopher or else that of a layman."[1] One must continually focus on improving character to become the best person possible. The time spent as a junior officer is an excellent opportunity to grow and develop one's character. We owe this continued growth and development to both those we lead and to ourselves.

Another aspect of developing character is the experience of failure. At one time or another, all junior officers will fail—regardless of their background and education. This failure can be something small, such as a division failing their inspections, or larger, like a newly commissioned ensign conning a ship at night. Stockdale said, "The challenge of education is not to prepare people for success but to prepare them for failure."[2] Failure is the crucible in which character is developed, and that is where leaders are forged. Stockdale went on to say, "I think that it's in hardship and failure that the heroes and the bums really get sorted out."[3] Failure is only negative if chosen to be viewed that way; otherwise, failure can be used as a means to improve oneself. It provides a chance to grow and develop character, especially under the guidance of a mentor.

Mentorship is essential for leadership development, and within the Stoic tradition mentorship is critical. In the beginning of *Meditations*, Roman emperor Marcus Aurelius, one of the greatest military leaders of the Roman Empire, attributed all of his good characteristics and values to his mentors who taught him.[4] All leaders, especially junior officers, should have such mentors. Mentorship is immensely valuable in passing along wisdom and experience to others, with Epictetus writing, "One of the best ways to elevate your character immediately is to find worthy role models to emulate."[5] Mentorship allows us to further develop our leadership and character by evaluating our decisions and discussing our faults openly without embarrassment.

To What End?

Leading sailors is a difficult task—one that requires fortitude and preparation. Junior officers are the first step in the officer chain of command for young sailors and are directly in the spotlight. Stoic leadership ensures that junior officers will lead well. Specifically, Stoicism is beneficial in three areas: It provides the ability to focus on what one can and cannot control, promotes and encourages discipline, and allows junior officers to maintain professionalism at all times.

Although it is often stereotyped as a cold philosophy that eliminates emotions, in essence Stoicism concerns itself with realizing what one can control and accepting the things one cannot. Stockdale said, "Uniquely to the Stoic, the only good things of absolute value are those that lie within the control of his will." For an officer, the externals could be deployment schedules, promotions, and orders from a superior. The internals that can be controlled are behavior, the training and readiness of subordinates, and job performance. We cannot control the actions of foreign countries or even of our own politicians. We may influence events, but they are not directly under anyone's control. However, the duty of commissioned officers dictates that we perform our jobs to the best of our ability for the defense of the nation and that we have the utmost control over ourselves.

Stoicism rests on a foundation of discipline, which is the cord that binds together leadership and followership. Without discipline, one can neither lead nor be led. Leadership through Stoicism requires us to maintain discipline over our emotions and actions. Epictetus wrote, "Evil is a by-product of forgetfulness, laziness, or distraction: it arises when we lose sight of our true aim in life." All militaries are effective because of discipline. The decline of the Roman army was largely due to the decline of discipline within the ranks. Discipline begins with the most senior officer and ends with the most junior sailor. We cannot expect our own subordinates to exercise discipline if we have none. In his *Discourses,* Epictetus states, referring to soldiers, that "[i]f you neglect your responsibilities when some severe order is laid upon you, do you not understand to what a pitiful state you bring the army in so far as in you lies?"[6] Stoic leadership ensures that we exercise discipline over ourselves first and our subordinates second.

Professionalism is the heart of a naval officer's career, and the ability to master one's emotions allows professionalism to flourish. Breaches of professionalism often result from an excess of negative emotions such as hatred, envy, fear, and greed. Stoicism calls for the control of one's emotions, and Stockdale noted that "the Stoic thinks of emotions as an act of will."[7] This eliminates the notion that the inner self is not under one's control, allowing for the proper execution of leadership and ensuring professionalism is maintained. A pilot cannot properly execute his mission if he is deathly afraid of being shot down. Viewing emotions as an act of will allows a military leader to control his or her emotions and lead in times of crisis, and to lead morally in times of peace. One must properly control one's emotions in order to keep one's professionalism consistent and high.

Levels of Leadership

A strong senior leader is necessary for any unit, but one person cannot completely control everything. A ship's captain cannot possibly dictate to every subordinate how specifically to do a job. In his book, *Turn the Ship Around*, Captain Marquet describes his leadership philosophy behind commanding the USS *Santa Fe*, pointing to a leader-leader structure that ensures leadership at every level of the chain of command. Using this philosophy, Marquet was able to take the poorest-performing submarine in the Navy and transform the *Santa Fe* into one of the highest performing.[8] Captain Rinn of the *Samuel B. Roberts* also utilized aspects of this philosophy, which led to his crew properly handling the damage-control situations after the ship struck a mine in the Persian Gulf. The *Samuel B. Roberts* was able to successfully clear the minefield while remaining prepared to fight—without any loss of life. Both Captains Marquet and Rinn were able to recognize that they could only do so much by themselves and empowered their crews.

An important aspect of junior-officer leadership is the ability to lead those who are beside them. Here, Stoic leadership is invaluable. A junior officer needs to recognize two separate issues. First, he or she is only fully in control of his or her actions. Second, a junior officer's reputation is not decided by the officer but by others. These two separate issues play a large role in peer leadership.

Junior officers must be in the utmost control of their own actions, as they influence the reputation of the naval services and their peers. However, there is a tendency to be influenced by group behavior, which can be either positive or negative. Every junior officer's action contributes to group behavior, and all must be on guard to ensure those actions positively influence their peers. The best leadership guidance is often through example.

Second, junior officers should not excessively worry about reputation, as they have little control over it. Instead, they should concentrate on acting honorably and their reputation will follow. Epictetus wrote, "Let the quality of your deeds speak on your behalf. We can't control the impressions others form about us, and the effort to do so only debases our character."[9] A virtuous person will have a virtuous reputation, but one without virtue will have a negative reputation. Worrying about reputation will make one want to be liked and may lead to bad decisions. As officers, our duty is not to be liked. Instead, our duty is to ensure the right path is taken.

Being a naval officer is a life-changing experience. We have the possibility to influence and lead. Doing so virtuously allows for the ability to not only change our lives but to change the lives of others. This is a great responsibility, and we must lead with a sense of duty. This requires character, strength, and perseverance. We control the fate of our nation and the fate of those under us. However, we are not the first to lead, and can find guidance from such leaders as Vice Admiral Stockdale, Captain Rinn, Captain Marquet, and Epictetus. With their guidance, junior officers can become great leaders and perform their duty for their country.

The concepts of Stoic leadership can help everyone lead, especially junior officers. An excellent example of someone who embodied character and leadership is Lieutenant Michael Murphy. After goat herders discovered his unit in the mountains of Afghanistan, he chose to let the herders go free even though they had compromised his position. He made this decision—which would cost him and two subordinates their lives—with the knowledge that he was fighting for the principles he believed in. While he and his team were surrounded by the enemy, he walked into a field of fire to meet his death so he could call for help for his men.

Such a sacrifice demonstrates the moral selflessness that all leaders should have. Heroes and leaders emerge in times of crisis and trouble. Military leaders should not be afraid of death, and those who have the courage to overcome and control the fear of death are true masters of their fate, and even death cannot overcome them. Vice Admiral Stockdale spoke truly when he said, "I concluded in prison that the pincers of fear and guilt are the destroyers of men. Nothing else."[10]

Ensign Burroughs graduated from the U.S. Naval Academy as a surface warfare officer and currently serves on board the USS *Freedom* (LCS-1) as a division officer.

Notes

1. James B. Stockdale, *Thoughts of a Philosophical Fighter Pilot* (Stanford, CA: Hoover Institution Press, 1995), 180.
2. Stockdale, *Thoughts of a Philosophical Fighter Pilot*, 220.
3. Ibid.
4. Marcus Aurelius, *Meditations*, trans. George Long (New York: Barnes and Noble, 2003), Chapter 1.
5. Epictetus, *Art of Living: The Classical Manual on Virtue, Happiness, and Effectiveness*, ed. Sharon Lebell (New York: HarperOne, 2007), 60.
6. Stockdale, *Thoughts of a Philosophical Fighter Pilot*, 189.
7. Ibid., 181.
8. David L. Marquet, *Turn the Ship Around!: A True Story of Turning Followers into Leaders* (New York: Portfolio 2012), xxvii.
9. Epictetus, *Art of Living*, 58.
10. Stockdale, *Thoughts of a Philosophical Fighter Pilot*, 218.

25 "LEADERSHIP FORUM: MORAL LEADERSHIP"

VADM James B. Stockdale, USN (Ret.)

There are many types of leaders and many styles of leadership. Drawing on wide reading in literature and philosophy and coupled with his own experience of eight years as a prisoner of war, Vice Admiral Stockdale writes about manipulation and extortion with respect to leadership. He contends that the antidote to both of these is moral virtue. He recognizes diversity in individual leaders but argues that "all styles must be built on moral virtue." He then explains what he means by the term and how it specifically relates to leadership. For Vice Admiral Stockdale, true leadership is inseparable from ethics and integrity.

"LEADERSHIP FORUM: MORAL LEADERSHIP"

By VADM James B. Stockdale, USN (Ret.), U.S. Naval Institute *Proceedings* (September 1980): 86–89.

> *"The extortion system, powered by our enemy's willingness to torture and impose isolation, quickly drove to the surface issues of moral integrity which at the pace of normal life could take years to fester and erupt into public view."*

Extortion, the squeeze-play drawing out of victims by force or compulsion, is dramatized in Godfather movies as an easily recognized, explicit, usually illegal way of conducting business. In reality, though, it is conducted much more frequently in subtler ways—ways which are both more difficult to recognize and more difficult to deal with. And by no means are these ways illegal, at least not in the sense that I use the word. We frequently face extortionary pressures in our everyday life, for extortion is just a concentrated form of manipulation through the use of fear and guilt. We who are in hierarchies—be they academic, business, military, or some other sort—are always in positions in which people are trying to manipulate us, to get moral leverage on us. It is the wise leader who comes to the conclusion that he can't be had if he can't be made to feel guilty. That is as true today in a free environment as it was for me during my years in prison camp. You have got to keep yourself clean—never do or say anything of which you can be made to be ashamed—in order to avoid being manipulated. A smart man, an ethical man, never gives a manipulator an even break. He is always prepared to quench the extortionist's artful insinuation of guilt with the icewater of a truthful, clear-conscienced put-down. The more benign the environment, the more insidious is the extortionist's style. "Then Arthur learned," says the legend, "as all leaders are astonished to learn, that peace, not war, is the destroyer of men; that tranquility, rather than danger, is the mother of cowardice; and that not need, but plenty, brings apprehension and unease."

This is not to suggest that there is only one way to lead, one manner of leadership, one style that best fits all circumstances. Of course not. I have merely said that all styles must be built on moral virtue. On specific leadership styles, I learned much from a talk by a psychoanalyst named Michael Maccoby. With a comprehensive understanding of American history, and after in-depth interviews of more than 200 American leaders of the 1970s, Maccoby concluded that there were four dominant leadership styles in the American past.

Now there are two things to remember as I quickly go over this analysis of Maccoby's. First of all, examples of men who embody each style have always been around and are still around; it's just that the challenges of different historic periods seemed to draw out particular types of leaders. And second, don't look for progress in leadership styles as we walk through this analysis. The leaders as leaders or as men don't get better as we follow the historic process.

From the Declaration of Independence until the credit system started to grow in the 1870s after the Civil War, most American leaders fell into a category he calls "craftsmen." They were "do-it-yourself" guys: self-reliant, strong-willed, cautious, suspicious, harder on themselves than they are on others. Benjamin Franklin was cited as their prototype then, Aleksandr Solzhenitsyn now. Their target of competition was not other men, but rather their idea of their own potential. Craftsmen climbed ladders not to get ahead of others, but to achieve that level of excellence they believed they had within themselves. They are mountain climbers, not players of what systems analysts call "zero-sum-games." They liked to make up their own minds; they did not buy school solutions. Craftsmen were men of conscience.

The industrial revolution and the need of its necessary credit and banking base were met by a new breed of leaders: Maccoby called them the "jungle fighters." Jungle fighters played "zero-sum-games" with gusto; there was just so much business out there and these were the men who knew how to stake out territory and get it. Andrew Carnegie, the steel magnate, was the prototype. Like craftsmen, jungle fighters were also men of conscience. Although they could sit at the board of directors table and figuratively decapitate incompetents with aplomb, they grieved. Characteristically they did not dodge issues; they settled scores eyeball to eyeball, tasting not only the self-satisfaction of authority but also the agony of pity.

After World War I, as the giant businesses the jungle fighters had built became bureaucracies, and as this "public relations" grew into an everyday national preoccupation, those jungle fighters were gradually displaced by the smoother "organization men." Like the jungle fighters, the organization men were paternalistic and authoritarian. But unlike those in pioneers of industry and finance who were motivated primarily by competitive zeal, "organization men," our psychoanalyst believes, were more motivated by a fear of failure. They were, nevertheless, characteristically honest; they were cautious men of conscience. They looked men in the eye when they fired them. They were "men of the heart," possessing qualities with an emotional content: a sense of commitment, loyalty, humor, and spontaneity.

In the early 1960s, a fourth style emerged to take the prominent leadership role. Maccoby identifies practitioners of this style as "the gamesmen." The gamesmen, impatient under the yoke of their paternalistic and authoritarian bosses, and educated more often than not in game-theory-oriented business schools, turned over a new page in leadership practices. The gamesmen believe that if one properly analyzes the "game" of life, the "game" of management, the "game" of leadership, one sees that it is not necessary to frame the problem as a "zero-sum-game." Rather, in their minds, American life can be as a "game" in which any number can play and win.

These gamesmen were relaxed, objective, open-minded, detached, cerebral swingers. Such emotional baggage as commitment or conscience they deemed inefficient and unnecessary. "Play your cards rationally to win and go to bed and sleep like a baby bothered without remorse." Some bothered with love and families; many gave them a tentative try and quit when they found them too burdensome. Maccoby said that there was a theatrical production that typified the leaders of each of these four ages and that the drama of the gamesmen was portrayed in the movie *The Sting*. You might remember that screenplay; in it, fair, competitive cooperative swingers, with the aid of teamwork and technology, destroyed the hung-up, authoritarian "Godfather."

The gamesmen, concluded psychoanalyst Maccoby, were basically "men of the head": cool intellectual types, walking calculating machines. "Men of the head" do many things well, but often have trouble coping with unpleasantness. These self-confident, cool, flexible men don't like to discipline people, they don't like to look people in the eye when they fire them. Moreover, they often crave to be loved, and that is a great leadership weakness. True leaders must be willing to stake out territory and identify and declare enemies. They must be fair and they may be compassionate, but they cannot be addicted to being loved by everybody. The man who has to be loved is an extortionist's dream. That man will do anything to avoid face-to-face unpleasantness; often he will sell his soul for praise. He can be had.

It was in the heyday of these gamesmen that some of their number, the cool, glib, analytical, cerebral so-called defense intellectuals took charge of the Pentagon under the direction of Robert Strange McNamara. At that juncture, I was fortunate enough to take a two-year sabbatical from military service for study at Stanford University. It was there that I started asking myself what truly rules the world: sentiment, efficiency, honor, justice?

The educated man, particularly the educated leader, copes with the fact that life is not fair. The problem for education is not to teach people how to deal with success but how to deal with failure. And the way to deal with failure is not to invent scapegoats or to lash out at your followers. Moreover, a properly educated leader, especially when harassed and under pressure, will know from his study of history and the classics that circumstances very much like those he is encountering have occurred from time to time on this earth since the beginning of history. He will avoid the self-indulgent error of seeing himself in a predicament so unprecedented, so unique, as to justify his making an exception to law, custom, or morality in favor of himself. The making of such exceptions has been the theme of public life throughout much of our lifetimes. For 20 years, we've been surrounded by gamesmen unable to cope with the wisdom of the ages. They make exceptions to law and custom in favor of themselves because they choose to view ordinary dilemmas as unprecedented crises.

Of course, it has been generally toward the above issue that I directed a course at the Naval War College. My formula for attacking this problem—both at the War College and in my present assignment at The Citadel—is the assignment of enough hard-core philosophy (*The Book of Job*, the Socratic dialogues of Plato, some of Aristotle's *Nicomachean Ethics*, Epictetus' *Enchiridion*, enough of Immanuel Kant to understand his concept of duty) and the reading of enough high-quality ultimate situation literature (Feodor Dostoyevsky's *House of the Dead*, Albert Camus's *Plague*, Joseph Conrad's *Typhoon*, and Herman Melville's

Billy Budd) as to deter self-pity when in extremis. With philosophy as the parent discipline, a discussion of courage might be focused on the writer who most thoroughly treated it, Aristotle. This might lead to the question of the validity of his viewpoint that courage is impossible in the absence of fear, that courage might be defined as a measure of how well one handles fear. How about the relationship between fear and imagination? Conrad has one of his characters state that imagination is the mother of fear. Must not a leader have imagination? If that breeds fear, might that not sap his courage? He surely must have courage above all else . . . etc. From such readings and discussions come understandings and clarifications of those elements of leadership which served in antiquity and those which must serve now.

Leadership must be based on goodwill. Goodwill does not mean posturing and, least of all, pandering to the mob. It means obvious and wholehearted commitment to the helping followers. We are tired of leaders we fear, tired of leaders we love, and most tired of leaders who let us take liberties with them. What we need for leaders are men of the heart who are so helpful that they, in effect, do away with the need of their jobs. But leaders like that are never out of a job, never out of followers. Strange as it sounds, great leaders gain authority by giving it away.

I am firmly convinced that the time I spent at Stanford has been a major force in molding my own personality as a leader. And I am just as firmly convinced that education in the classics and in the principles of human relationships gave me far better preparation for being a prisoner of war than did the traditional survival and evasion training. My ideas on the art of moral leadership received their most profound testing in the stress and degradation—yes, in the extortion environment—of a Communist prisoner of war camp.

The intensity and stark drama of my eight years in North Vietnam provided a quantity and range of leadership challenge that would more than fill an ordinary lifetime. In mere months or weeks, men made and destroyed their reputations. Those behind bars seemed to be scanning reams of data on the problems of good and evil in fast time. The extortion system, powered by our enemy's willingness to torture and impose isolation, quickly drove to the surface issues of moral integrity which at the pace of normal life could take years to fester and erupt into public view.

For united resistance, men had to get on quickly with the business of assimilating knowledge of the character traits of their fellow prisoners. This knowledge had to be more penetrating and more calculating than the sort commonly found sufficient for amicable social life out here in freedom. Is the newcomer emotionally stable? (We had to make a good guess as to whether he had the steadfastness and composure to warrant being trusted with secret material in that torture environment.) Does he have moral integrity? In the privacy of the torture room, will he go to the wall in silence, or do what is so commonplace in the business world nowadays and try to make a deal? Is he sophisticated enough to avoid falling for the interrogator's bait? Will he work his way out on a limb by "gabbing" after that clever interrogator has dangled before him such American-life enticements as: Let us reason together; You are a pragmatic people, meet us halfway?

In the extortion environment one can always better his own position at the expense of his fellows by holding still for the manipulator's setting up of subtle compromises. A loner makes out by making acknowledged or tacit deals. This will never do. The intensity of life in jail clearly illuminated for us prisoners of war the truth that for the greatest good for the greatest number of us, for our maximum happiness, maximum self-respect, maximum protection of one another, each of us had to submerge our individual survival instincts into an ideal of universal solidarity. "No deals" and "Unity over self" became our mottos.

Some of you are doubtless skeptical of the practicability of such ideals which seem to ask more of a man than human nature might be thought to allow. To the skeptics let me say right off that when there is leadership by example, and when there is a commonly shared threat of total estrangement and humiliation, united magnanimous behavior can become a reality. When a man looks at the bottom of the barrel through creeping and growing fissures in the thin veneer of civilization that coats his existence, he suddenly realizes that his slip back into barbarism could come about in weeks. As he peers over the edge of his world, it dawns on him how lonesome and terrible it would be down there without communication, friends, or common cultural ties. He vividly realizes how men, fellow countrymen, need one another for understanding and for sanity. As he sees himself clinging to a receding civilization with his fingernails, it becomes clear to him that "No deals" and "Unity over self" are not goody-goody idealistic slogans; rather they are practical guides to action.

We saw that we had to build and tend our own civilization if we were to keep ourselves from becoming animals. A man must relate to a community, a commonality of communication style, a commonality of ritual, of laws, of traditions, of poetry, of shared dreams, if he is to prevail, if he is to resist. "Man does not live by bread alone." Learning the truth and full meaning of that biblical adage was lesson number one for us in that crucible of pressure. It goes without saying that the first job of leadership is to provide the communication necessary for that civilization, that ritual, those laws, those traditions.

The problem was to improvise a communications system for a prison camp in which everybody lived in solitary confinement, a solitary confinement in silence, a solitary confinement in which the use of torture was considered just punishment for those who break that silence to communicate with their fellows. Our Vietnam enemies gave us two ways to go on this. We could lie low and not communicate and go to seed over the years of silence and solitude. (One starts "looking for a friend" after a couple of years.) Or we could communicate as a matter of duty and take our lumps. Since the dictates of conscience and morality made the latter the only way to go, the problem became how to communicate stealthily. For us, trapped in isolation in Hanoi, the means for that communication was a tap code that would break through the walls of solitary confinement, the walls of silence. (For the mechanics of the code, I suggest reading Commander Everett Alvarez's "Sound: A POW's Weapon," pages 91–93 in the August 1976 *Proceedings*.)

Leadership basics are vividly portrayed in the prison camp example. Prison serves as a useful "test bed" (to use a test pilot expression) in which to study in detail man's behavior under stress, stress of the sort under which many of life's crucial decisions are necessarily made. Mark this down in your book as lesson two: in the high-stress situation, "status" will not carry you as a leader. That is to say, you have to have more going for you than your title, your seniority, your position in your hierarchy, your rank. You cannot get by with performing like a quarterback who is functional only while being protected "in the pocket"; you've got to be able to scramble and improvise, on your feet, and alone. Even this assumes that by the time the pressure is on, you would have earned your followers' respect, and not just their fear or friendship. Unless people respect you as a leader, when the fat is in the fire they'll just listen to your orders and calmly walk away.

Lesson three: under stress, ordinary "transactional" leadership will never cut it. That is to say, transactional leadership propelled simply by the effect of give and take, leadership driven by the base instincts of the marketplace and bargaining table whereby the leader makes an accommodation in the expectation that his followers will make a complementary accommodation, simply will not stand up. This may come as news to you because the "transactional" leader/follower relationship is so much a part of our way of doing business in everyday economic, social, even academic life. But what to us is the ordinary dance of life, the dance propelled by continuous compromise, finds itself floundering under pressure. Inputs are needed from "transforming" leaders. Transforming leaders don't simply analyze what they think their people want and then try to give them part of it and hope they will receive a counter accommodation in return. Transforming leaders instruct and inspire their followers to recognize worthy needs, and they make those needs their wants. They have a way of raising their followers out of their everyday selves and into their better selves, of making them conscious of the high-minded goals that lie unconscious beneath their self-centered desires. In summary, the transforming leader has the wisdom to read the minds of his flock, to understand what they want, to know what they ought to want; and he has the persuasive power to implant the latter into their hearts.

In all that I have been saying, I've made the points that leaders under pressure must keep themselves absolutely clean morally (the relativism of the social sciences will never do). They must lead by example, must be able to implant high-mindedness in their followers, must have competence beyond status, and must have earned their followers' respect by demonstrating integrity. What I've been describing as the necessary leadership attributes under pressure are the bedrock virtues all successful leaders must possess, "under pressure and otherwise." Prison was just the "test bed," just the meat-grinder that vividly illuminated these prime building blocks for me.

INDEX

ABOUT THE EDITOR

Timothy J. Demy is professor of military ethics at the U.S. Naval War College. Prior to his appointment he served as a Navy chaplain for twenty-seven years. He has authored and edited books on ethics, theology, and current issues and contributed to numerous journals and encyclopedias. He served as the American managing editor of the international *Journal of Military Ethics.*

The Naval Institute Press is the book-publishing arm of the U.S. Naval Institute, a private, nonprofit, membership society for sea service professionals and others who share an interest in naval and maritime affairs. Established in 1873 at the U.S. Naval Academy in Annapolis, Maryland, where its offices remain today, the Naval Institute has members worldwide.

Members of the Naval Institute support the education programs of the society and receive the influential monthly magazine *Proceedings* or the colorful bimonthly magazine *Naval History* and discounts on fine nautical prints and on ship and aircraft photos. They also have access to the transcripts of the Institute's Oral History Program and get discounted admission to any of the Institute-sponsored seminars offered around the country.

The Naval Institute's book-publishing program, begun in 1898 with basic guides to naval practices, has broadened its scope to include books of more general interest. Now the Naval Institute Press publishes about seventy titles each year, ranging from how-to books on boating and navigation to battle histories, biographies, ship and aircraft guides, and novels. Institute members receive significant discounts on the Press's more than eight hundred books in print.

Full-time students are eligible for special half-price membership rates. Life memberships are also available.

For a free catalog describing Naval Institute Press books currently available, and for further information about joining the U.S. Naval Institute, please write to:

Member Services
U.S. NAVAL INSTITUTE
291 Wood Road
Annapolis, MD 21402-5034
Telephone: (800) 233-8764
Fax: (410) 571-1703
Web address: www.usni.org